Labor Union Representatives

Other books by Walt Baer

Labor Relations for the Practitioner
(McFarland, 1989)

Collective Bargaining: Custom and Practice
(McFarland, 1989)

Arbitration for the Practitioner
(McFarland, 1988)

Winning in Labor Arbitration
(Crain Books, 1982)

The Operating Manager's Labor Relations Guidebook
(Kendall/Hunt, 1978)

Strikes
(American Management Association, 1975)

The Labor Arbitration Guide
(Dow Jones–Irwin, 1974)

Practice and Precedent in Labor Relations
(Lexington Books, 1972)

Discipline and Discharge Under the Labor Agreement
(American Management Association, 1972)

Grievance Handling: 101 Guides for Supervisors
(American Management Association, 1970)

LABOR UNION
REPRESENTATIVES
Allowed and Prohibited Practices

by
Walt Baer

McFarland & Company, Inc., Publishers
Jefferson, North Carolina, and London

British Library Cataloguing-in-Publication data are available

Library of Congress Cataloguing-in-Publication Data

Baer, Walt
   Labor union representatives : allowed and prohibited practices /
by Walt Baer.
     p. cm.
   Includes index.
     ISBN 0-89950-637-2 (lib. bdg. : 55# alk. paper) ∞
     1. Shop stewards – United States. 2. Shop stewards – Legal status,
laws, etc. – United States. 3. Trade unions – United States –
Officials and employees. 4. Trade unions – Officials and employees –
Legal status, laws, etc. – United States. 5. Trade unions – United
States – Organizing. I. Title.
HD6490.S52U63 1992
331.87'33 – dc20   91-52752
                                                                         CIP

Manufactured in the United States of America

McFarland & Company, Inc., Publishers
  Box 611, Jefferson, North Carolina 28640

To Janet,
the answer to
my life's prayers

Contents

Contents

Preface

Some believe unions are on their way out. Don't you believe it. They are still vigorous and active and ever restless in their quest for the representation of still more groups of employees.

And the labor-management relationship continues to be the largest single issue on corporate management's agenda.

In a previous book, *Grievance Handling: 101 Guides for Supervisors,* I undertook to present a comprehensive survey of the numerous and various problem areas encountered by management in its administration of the grievance procedure in the collective bargaining agreement. That study was intended to fill a gap that existed in the technical literature and concurrently to throw some light on the impact of management errors in the administration of this contractual provision. Although it was designed primarily for supervisors, personnel managers, and industrial-relations personnel, I believed that such a study might be of interest to all those individuals who represented labor and management in their relationships with each other.

In this book, I attempt to present a comprehensive review of the numerous and various problem areas encountered by both union and management members in their relationships with each other and in their administration of the union collective bargaining agreement. This study is intended to fill a gap that exists in the technical literature and also to throw some light on the possible impact of management errors in the handling of union representatives and in the administration of the union contract.

Although it was designed primarily for supervisors, personnel managers, and industrial relations personnel, I believe this study will also be of interest to *all* of those individuals representing labor and management on both sides of the table. It is my impression that no one has to urge one's contemporaries to concern themselves with this area, which is so vital to their respective roles and interests.

With the growing sensitivity to and sophistication in the field of labor-management relations, additional studies in many segments of labor relations are sorely needed. It is with one such issue that the present study is concerned. This is quite different from the aforementioned book in that it deals with a specific problem area, one of the more sensitive and troublesome areas between the parties. Concern for the fact that management's relationship with the union officials representing its employee's interests often raises the most difficult questions with regard to their respective rights, duties, and obligations was the motivation for this study. No one can deny the legitimacy of this concern. These confrontations raise with particular insistence the perennial questions mentioned above.

This volume does not pretend to give all the answers, nor do I wish to plead the cause of "solution." But I am optimistic enough to believe that a serious examination of the several issues reviewed here may not be a complete waste of time for the practitioner and student. Sufficient reasons, of which this search is one, may be revealed to make such interested individuals more concerned and introspective about their roles, obligations, and responsibilities.

This book is written to provide valuable insights into the latitude and freedom allowed union representatives under the labor agreement and applicable laws. It is also a source to begin research for the practitioner faced with the preparation of an arbitration case. Finally, it might serve as the foundation for a pertinent and meaningful module in a supervisor's labor-relations training program.

I have tried to be objective and impartial throughout, favoring neither labor nor management. The views expressed here are my interpretations of case decisions. Coverage has been given to arbitrators whose views do not coincide in every particular, but it was felt that the interested reader would benefit from a recognition of the fact that even experts on a difficult subject such as this still have some differences of opinion.

About the Author

Walt Baer has a B.S. in psychology from Youngstown University and an M.S. in clinical psychology from the University of Pittsburgh. With over 35 years of industrial relations experience, he started his career as an international staff representative with the United Steelworkers Union. His management experience includes positions as vice president for personnel and industrial relations with TBC, vice president for human resources with UNC Resources Inc., vice president of industrial relations for Peabody Coal Company, corporate director for industrial relations with Samsonite Corporation, corporate labor specialist for Brunswick Corporation, and as a mediator with the Federal Conciliation Service. He also has been a psychological counselor, labor-management consultant, arbitrator, lecturer and seminar leader. Baer is the author of 12 industrial relations textbooks and over 100 articles in professional journals.

Chapter 1
The Dual Role

It should be realized that *the union representative actually functions in a dual capacity.* On the one hand, he is customarily a bargaining-unit employee who holds some hourly productive task in a job classification requiring that a certain set of duties and functions be performed. When functioning in this worker capacity, he naturally is governed by the same rules and regulations governing behavior and conduct of other unit employees – for example, attendance, lateness, output, effort, etc. However, when operating in the role of union representative, he dons a cloak which provides him with a certain degree of immunity from management's discipline and orders, and his conduct and behavior are measured by a different yardstick. As an advocate for his special-interest group, he must enjoy a certain latitude to represent his constituents vigorously and carry out the duties of his office.

For these reasons, one of the questions often present when management disciplines a union representative for alleged misconduct is whether the individual was functioning as a union representative or as an employee under the labor agreement. Another question which frequently arises concerns the extent to which the company has the right to discipline an employee while he is operating as a union official. Trying to bring the point into sharper focus, let us imagine that a union official instigates, aids, or participates in an unlawful work stoppage in violation of a no-strike article. Although he was functioning as a union representative, it is clear that management would be justified to impose discipline, notwithstanding the fact that he was functioning in his official union capacity. And in many cases where union officials are involved in this kind of outlaw activity, the supreme penalty under the labor agreement, discharge, is often applied by the company.

On the other hand, suppose the union representative is argumentative, adversarial, or somewhat belligerent in his relations with management during grievance proceedings. The imposition of discipline for behavior of that type has to be very carefully considered by arbitrators

1

and should be considered equally as carefully by management representatives considering discipline, or unwise awards by arbitrators considering such actions could undermine the collective-bargaining relationship
by unreasonably restraining union representatives in the pursuit and ad-
vocacy of their union responsibilities.

Ordinarily, an employee's refusal to obey the order of a management
representative would constitute insubordination and properly result in
some discipline action being taken against the employee. But suppose the
order issued by management is to a union president directing him to attend, or not to attend, a labor-management meeting. It has been held
that under such circumstances, an employer does not have the right to
impose a disciplinary suspension upon the union president since the
order had to do with the employee's status as a union officer rather than
an employee. The impropriety of the discipline was indicated by several
factors: (1) The union president was not contractually obliged to attend
all meetings called by the company, and his refusal to do so here violated
no other contract provisions. (2) The president's refusal did not prohibit
the holding of the meeting, since it was held and other union committee
members did attend. (3) The president presented a reason for not attending the meeting at the time it was scheduled, and the company failed to
show that the reason given had been frivolous. (4) The union is entitled
to its legitimate concern regarding when meetings with the employer are
scheduled. To hold otherwise would enable the company to compel a
union officer's attendance at any and every meeting scheduled by the
employer, irrespective of the circumstances, and the union could be
hindered in effectively performing its proper collective-bargaining functions under the agreement.[1]

Under another agreement, a union president was discharged for
chronic absenteeism and tardiness. This action was taken pursuant to
and in accord with a plant rule, following the issuance by management
of several prior warnings to the employee. The company contended it
had finally instituted this action because of the excessive number of un-
reported absences, which constituted about 25 percent of his working
time lost for this reason, and all prior management efforts to correct his
behavior had failed. However, since the majority of his occasions of
absences and tardiness apparently were necessitated by *legitimate* union
business and the remaining number of his absences were not sufficient
to constitute a case for chronic absenteeism, the arbitrator ordered his
reinstatement and awarded back pay for 75 percent of the lost time on
the basis of the union president's prior attendance at work.[2]

The above case provides a couple of interesting points worthy of
mention. First, in such a case, it is always advisable for the employer to

establish as accurately as possible the actual reasons for the employee's absences. A second consideration must always be the extent of the freedom and latitude accorded to union representatives by the language of the labor agreement. In some instances, the first consideration may intermingle with the second consideration and provide management with indications of whether such absenteeism or tardiness may be sanctioned by the contract. The other point to be commented upon here is the judgment of the arbitrator in this situation. It is a well-established principle among the overwhelming majority of arbitrators that an employee owes his *first* consideration *to his employer* and *to his task within the bargaining unit,* his obligations to his union duties coming *second.* Unless the contract deals with some allowance of time for union officials to engage in official union activity, thus allowing him to be frequently absent on union business to the neglect of his work assignments, most arbitrators would expect the employee to give first attention to his employer.

A different result was obtained when a company disciplined a grievance committeeman who began working on his own grievances after being told to report to his work assignment. Despite the order, the employee continued to work on his grievances, with the exception of a few minutes spent on telephone calls relating to other union matters. He continued this activity for two hours, during which time he was directed to report for work not less than six times by three responsible supervisors. The union contended that the company had discriminated against the grievant for union activity under the agreement. The company contended he had been discharged for his refusal to carry out the lawful order of his supervisors. Secondly, they contended that the union had failed to prove that the grievant's union activities on the day in question or prior thereto had had any relationship to his discharge.

The language of the contract between the parties was silent with respect to under what circumstances members of the grievant committee could work on union matters, including preparation of grievances. However, it was clearly established that by custom and practice, members of the grievance committee did perform such union work at *any* time of the day or night and were merely required to notify their supervisors that they were taking time for the purpose of performing union duties. It is significant that while this was clearly a fact, it was also a fact that regular employees were not similarly privileged to expend such time on union activities. Some comments of the arbitrator pertinent to this matter explain why he considered the individual's conduct as constituting insubordination:

The proper course of action by an employee is to perform the assigned duty and file a grievance to protest the alleged infringement of his right. The grievant seeks to distinguish his position from that of his fellow employees and cloak himself with the authority vested in him as a member of the grievance committee to work on *their* grievances at any time. In effect, he seeks for himself a privileged position unavailable to those who selected him to protect their rights under the collective bargaining agreement. *As an employee* of the company he should have responded to the orders issued to him by his supervisors and then filed a grievance as any other employee in a less privileged position would be required to do. The grievant knew he had 15 days during which to file his grievance and time was not of the essence.

Therefore, under the limited circumstances involved in this dispute, the board finds that the grievant was not engaged in bona fide union business *during the period of time he was engaged in the preparation and contemplation of his own grievances,* and his failure to report for work . . . constitutes at least passive resistance to the repeated orders of his supervisors.[3]

However, in view of this committeeman's good 13-year work record and the fact that the insubordination was more in the nature of passive resistance than an outright refusal to obey his employer's orders, the arbitrator reduced his discharge to a suspension without pay for a period of over three months.

You must search long and hard to discover a case where management has disciplined union representatives in which the union does not raise a claim of discrimination or union animus. And it is regrettably true that as a matter of general industrial-relations experience, some managements have a feeling of hostility toward individuals who serve as stewards and union representatives. Of course, for the union merely to raise such a claim in an arbitration hearing is simply to say it and not to establish it. But where arbitrators are faced with such union contentions, they naturally feel duty-bound to examine the evidence carefully to determine if the alleged reasons put forth by the company constitute just and proper cause for the discipline or discharge. Where the company's evidence supports and substantiates its action, in the absence of any odor of antiunionism, arbitrators will uphold management action taken against an employee–union representative.

A case which fits nicely the above-mentioned concept occurred where an employer discharged a union official for inefficiency and insubordination as an employee. The arbiter was able to uphold this management decision because the real evidence disclosed that the union official (1) had the poorest efficiency record of 250 employees whose work had been studied and compared with his; (2) despite several warnings from management, his work continued to be unsatisfactory to the time of his discharge; and (3) he admitted that during the week prior to his discharge, he refused to fill out his daily performance records, as required of all employees, despite specific instructions from his foreman that he must do so. His claim that his poor work record was due in part to his necessity for taking time-off to attend to union business was rejected. The evidence on this point showed that he had taken very little time for such purposes in the several months just prior to his discharge. The union's argument that his discharge for inefficiency should be found discriminatory was rejected since other employees who had even better efficiency records than the union official had been discharged by the company for the same reason of inefficiency.[4]

Although it is quite uncommon for a union to give management any voice in the selection of those officers who will represent it, it is not entirely unheard of. This, like most everything else in the field of labor relations, is a negotiable item, but under the law, it is not one the parties could bargain to an impasse over. However, if both parties are amenable to discussions on the matter, the ultimate result may be that one or both will give some voice, or veto power, to the other regarding its representational selections.

Under a contract which stated that the union would discuss the appointment of head shop stewards with the employer, the company was justified in refusing to recognize a particular individual under the circumstance surrounding her appointment.[5] The contract provided that the union "will not appoint or continue as head shop steward any individual whom management shows to be unacceptable because of irresponsibility, incompetence in his work, or other good cause." Management's objections to the individual appointed were rooted in her exercising her "forceful personality" improperly and interfering with management by directing the work of the employees. The arbitrator agreed, and evaluated that the employee's behavior and general incompatibility were readily recognizable as character or personality traits "that would impair, hinder, or prevent such a person from carrying out his duties and responsibilities as a union steward," at least for representing the union with management.

In another case, a union representative contended he was operating in his union capacity during an encounter with his supervisor regarding an order to return to work. It appears that rain had caused work to halt for about an hour, and when the rain had markedly slackened but not entirely stopped, the supervisor signaled all men to return to work. Of the 30–40 men involved, all responded to the signal and returned to work with the exception of the union official. He remained under shelter and made no attempt to discuss the matter with his foreman. In deciding this matter, the arbitrator commented:

> Quite aside from rejecting the grievant's belated and self-serving effort to explain away his behavior by saying he had put on his union hat as the general foreman approached, *the Umpire believes that it should also be noted that X's status as a Shop Steward did not, in any event, mean that he was immune from the obligation to obey reasonable orders* by his supervisor to return to work.[6]

It's apparent this was an instance where a union steward mistakenly assumed that his union office enabled him to disregard his obligations as an employee. Again, this arbitrator upheld management's action in docking the steward for the time he remained in the rain shelter refusing to return to work. It might even be reasonably argued that a stronger penalty could have been exacted here and upheld.

Section 9(a) of the National Labor Relations Act, as amended (29 U.S.C. 159), provides that representatives designated or selected for the purposes of collective bargaining by the majority of employees in the appropriate unit shall be the *exclusive* representatives of all employees in such unit for bargaining with respect to pay, wages, hours of employment, and other conditions of employment. This affirmative duty of the employer to bargain collectively with the chosen representative of his employees imposes a correlative duty not to bargain with any other employee representatives (*Medo Photo Supply Corp. v. NLRB*, 321 U.S. 678 [8 LC-51, 176] [1944]). In *Medo Photo Supply*, the Supreme Court said: "The National Labor Relations Act makes it the duty of the employer to bargain collectively with the chosen representatives of his employees. The obligation being exclusive, it exacts the negative duty to treat with no other."

Therefore, a supervisor, by ignoring the union as the employees' *exclusive* bargaining representative, by negotiating with employees concerning matters pertaining to the broad and general areas of wages, hours, and working conditions—or inducing employees to abandon the union by making promises of higher wages or better benefits—does so in violation of Section 8(1) of the act, which forbids interference with the right of employees to bargain collectively through representatives of *their* choice. It is a violation of the essential principle of collective bargaining and an infringement of the act when the agent of the employer disregards the bargaining representative by negotiating with individual employees, *whether a majority or a minority*, with respect to wages, hours, and working conditions. The statute guarantees to all employees the right to bargain collectively through their chosen representatives. Bargaining carried on by the employer's agents directly with the (whether a majority or a minority) who have not revoked their designation of a bargaining agent would be subversive of the mode of collective bargaining which the statute has ordained, as the National Labor Relations Board (NLRB) the authoritative body in this field, has often ruled. Such conduct is therefore an interference with the rights guaranteed by Section 7 and a violation of Section 8(1) of the act.

Acts of insubordination by two union officials resulted in their employer imposing a three-day disciplinary suspension upon each when they persisted in writing grievances in a locker-room rest area and refused to go to the foreman's office to write their grievances where their privacy had been assured. The restriction of this area was nothing new to either of them since the order barring the use of the locker room for such purposes had been in effect for almost a year. Despite the fact that the union representatives had clocked out and were acting as union officials, during which time they might not otherwise be required to obey an order which could interfere with the functioning of the grievance procedure, the company's action could not be said to have deprived the union of any of its substantive or procedural rights. The alternate areas suggested by the company did not prevent the union officials from pursuing the grievance to a final conclusion. This alternative area also did not impair their privacy or the freedom necessary to a full discussion and a writing of the grievance. Also of consequence was the consideration that the grievants were not ordered to stop processing the grievance, nor was the order related to production, and it could not be considered a sudden and arbitrary imposition of authority by the company. For these reasons, the arbitrator ruled for the employer.[7]

In still another case involving insubordinate conduct, an arbitrator ruled that a local union president should have signed an agreement to turn over to the employer any inventions, discoveries, or improvements pertaining to the employer's business – and then have filed a grievance protesting being forced to sign such agreement. Instead, the union official remained adamant in his refusal to sign. In this instance, the employer had made it clear that it intended to enforce a policy of requiring employees to sign a patent-disclosure agreement and that it would not accept such signed documents stating that the agreement had been signed "under protest." The arbitrator, however, fashioned an interesting remedy by ruling that the discharge of the union president be converted to suspension to last until the final disposition of the grievances which had been filed challenging the employer's rights to require the employees to sign the agreements as a condition of employment. At that time the president was to be reinstated without loss of seniority but without back pay.[8]

Another dispute dealt with the narrow and troublesome issue whether discharge is an appropriate penalty for the refusal to execute an order when it is determined that there was no proper basis upon which to issue the order. The arbiter found small consolation in knowing he was not the first to have to wrestle with this problem. At the Hegeler Zinc Co., arbitrator Alex Elsen found that "resort to the grievance procedure is not an antidote for pneumonia" and reinstated an employee who had refused to leave employment in a heated building to work outside in cold inclement weather.[9]

Arbiter Whitley McCoy, acknowledging he had frequently regarded insubordination as inexcusable, nevertheless reinstated a steward who had been discharged for refusal to comply with an unlawful order of his supervisor which would have prevented him from attending to legitimate union business in the plant.[10] The question in this case was whether under all the circumstances of the case there was provocation which justified the employee's refusal to do as he was directed merely because he felt that he had been dealt with harshly. The employee was a union steward and had been employed as a yard laborer for about seven years at the time of his discharge. He and another employee were given a work assignment which they obligingly went to and commenced in good order. However, in the course of it they encountered difficulty and told the foreman it was impossible for them to continue to perform the task satisfactorily because of impediments caused by other workmen. The foreman did not agree that the obstructions were sufficient to prevent the work's accomplishments. After an exchange of words in which the employee insisted he could not do the work while the foreman persisted that he could, he was finally told, "Well that's the only job I've got for you, and in that case you should punch your card." It was undisputed that after the union steward left, the foreman then asked the other employee whether he felt the same way about the job, whereupon that employee replied, "No, sir, I don't understand the job, but I want to work." The foreman then proceeded to instruct him on how to continue the work.

However, the grievant did not leave the premises but returned to the job after taking his tools to a toolhouse and picking up his personal effects. Passing by the job again, he indicated to the foreman that he would not punch out and leave unless he had an opportunity to discuss the matter with someone in management above the foreman. When he persisted in his refusal to leave after repeated requests that he do so, the foreman called the chief of plant protection, who escorted him from the plant. At the arbitration hearing, when questioned concerning the basis for the discharge, the foreman testified that the steward "was fired because he refused to take a direct order (to leave the plant) and because he was failing to do his work." He stated further that he was unable to say whether he would have recommended discharge based solely upon failure to do the work assigned.

Commenting on the evidence and giving his conclusions, the arbiter stated:

> A careful consideration of the entire case leads the arbitrator to the conclusion that facts presented here, while reflecting that B was being *wrongfully* sent home, *were nevertheless insufficient* to place the situation within that exceptional category where arbitrators have found that the order was so patently wrong or unlawful as to excuse non-compliance. This is not a case where the employee was goaded or provoked to the point that his flaunting of authority may be condoned. As a steward, B was especially charged with knowledge of appropriate remedial steps that he might pursue in an effort to redress the wrong which he felt was being done to him.[11]

So finding, the discharge of the steward was upheld for just cause.

Combining abuse of the special privileges accorded him as a union president with less than acceptable conduct as an employee ultimately produced the discharge of a union president. This union official's personal record listed instances of his failure or refusal to carry out work assignments, abuse of the permission granted by the agreement to confer with others in connection with union duties, failure to punch his time card as required by general plant rules when leaving the plant, leaving the plant without notice "while clocked-in," assigning work to other employees without authorization, holding unauthorized union meetings on plant property while on the clock, and failing to comply with plant rules regarding parking. This record culminated in a meeting between the employer, the union president, and the union's regional representative at which his prior unsatisfactory work and conduct were discussed and the company agreed to give him one more chance. One week after the meeting, he again failed to perform or improperly performed work assignments, left the plant one half hour early on one day, and failed to work on the last day during the week following the meeting. After four days of arbitration hearings and many days of contemplation, the arbitrator sustained the company's discharge action.[12]

The penalty of discharge has been sustained in a number of cases where union representatives were in direct violation of a no-strike provision in the applicable collective bargaining agreement, even though the agreement failed to specify such a penalty. A review of awards involving disciplinary action in connection with illegal strike activity reveals that decisions are not entirely consistent, and some appear to be based on sounder reasoning than others. However, it is possible to glean several general principles which can be applied to the facts of different cases. Of course, care must be exercised in recognizing the differences in the contract language which may be controlling in any particular case. A large number of such cases will be examined in detail later. Because of the dual role of the union representative as an employee and a union official, a brief sampling is in order here.

In a Fruehauf Trailer Co. case a discharge was upheld where a union committeeman ordered employees in his department to put away their tools and go home, the grievant departing with them.[13] In other cases involving such negative leadership, discharge action has been affirmed where a shop steward told the workmen to leave work and personally called a strike in violation of the terms of the contract.[14]

Where a shop steward was one of eight men who refused to work because of excessive heat and apparently led the recalcitrant group, or in any event was the one considered most responsible for this group action, discharge was sustained.[15]

In a dispute at Sherwin-Williams, discharge was upheld for four union officers who were instrumental in calling a continuous union meeting which lasted 10 days and personally passed out bills urging others to attend. The arbitrator in this matter found that such a meeting amounted to a strike in violation of the terms of the contract.[16] The same arbitral holding was obtained when a union stewardess brought the employees, who had stopped working, to the office of the plant manager instead of directing them to return to work.[17]

And the same was the result where a union president and a secretary-treasurer were discharged for leaving their jobs and refusing, along with others, to work under new company schedules. In this case, the union president refused to let the company's personnel director talk to the other workers alone, and there was further evidence that he actually led the stoppage. Despite the differences in the factual basis, the arbitrator affirmed both discharges.[18]

Typical of the union position in cases of this sort is the contention that in his capacity as a union official, their representative owes a duty *only* to the union. This argument continues that the company cannot legitimately interfere with the performance of this duty, and any control or domination exercised by the company could conceivably involve a violation of the unfair-practice provisions of the Labor Management Relations Act. According to the union, a company cannot properly complain about the way an employee carries out his union functions.

A minority of arbitrators concur with this concept. The majority hold that even though the union's representative is functioning in his official union capacity, his conduct may nevertheless subject him to discipline or discharge if it is in violation of an existing collective bargaining agreement or exceeds the boundaries of reasonable propriety of conduct. Like anyone else, a union official is subject to discharge or discipline for infractions directly related to his performance as an employee. As an employee, his duties and responsibilities are the same as any other bargaining-unit employee. The discharge of a union steward has also been held justified for refusing to do assigned work, which refusal resulted in a walkout, an outcome which the grievant had expected.[19]

The essence of such decisions is that the company cannot usually legitimately interfere with or direct the performance of the functions of an individual as a union official. The way an employee carries out this strictly union function, therefore, is normally not subject to censure by the employer in the absence of evidence of some improper activity or leadership which constitutes a breach of the terms of the agreement.[20]

In his book *Labor Management Contracts at Work* (Harper Bros., 1961) Morris Stone, editorial director of the American Arbitration Association, observed (at p. 66):

> When a steward or union officer is disciplined for violating some rule of conduct, there may be a dispute as to whether there was just cause for the penalty. To that extent a steward's case may be no different from that of any other employee. But when the union asserts that the disciplinary action was motivated by an attempt to frustrate collective bargaining, or that the steward's violation occurred during the course of negotiations and was, therefore, beyond the reach of the employer's power to discipline, a different sort of problem is present.

It would appear that in a case between General Electric and the UAW the company was trying scrupulously to avoid the slightest appearance that its suspension of a union official was for anything other than his repeated violation of conduct as an employee and not as a shop-committee chairman. Over a period of more than a year, management patiently tried to convince the union official voluntarily to stop diluting his production work slips by understating the time he spent on legitimate union activities. The labor agreement contained specific provisions relating to the time spent during working hours by union officers on union business and limited the amount of such time that would be paid for. Despite the company's reasonable protestations, the shop-committee chairman continued to mark on his production work slip time that he had actually been spending on union business which should have been reported on a separate slip. The result of his erroneous reporting gave a false picture of his productivity and could have caused inaccurate production records. When he persisted in this improper practice, the company finally suspended him for a one-week period.

The arbitrator concluded it could hardly be said that the company was trying to dissuade or discourage the grievant in his diligent pursuit of his important functions as the key representative of the union in the shop. Absent was any proof that the company ever withheld permission to leave his work area for union activities. Important under this agreement was the need to distinguish accurately between work time and grievance-handling time. This was implicit in the very nature of the contractual limitations, and obviously if there was a ceiling on the employer's requirement to pay for some union-activity time, the company had a right to insist that distinctions between work time and grievance time be correctly reflected on its time tickets.[21]

One of the functions of the union representative, usually one holding the rank of steward but others as well, from a practical standpoint is to discuss with management problems which might give rise to grievances or dissatisfactions within operating departments and to communicate in such a fashion that operations within the plant may be carried on smoothly and without disruptions or interruptions. Under the typical labor agreement, such union representatives do not have the right to leave their work and keep under surveillance other employees or members of management without having first obtained permission, usually from the supervisor. This is particularly so where the steward is being paid by the company to perform bargaining-unit work assigned to him. He certainly is not being paid to carry on union business which is not covered under the contract.

This was the precise situation where an arbitrator considered management justified in discharging a departmental steward who had left his work station without permission for the purpose of requesting a conference with his foreman concerning another employee's grievance. Controlling factors in this ruling: (1) The grievance did not actually require *immediate* processing and could have been reasonably delayed to a more appropriate time. (2) Under this agreement it was not the steward's function to request such a conference but the obligation of the aggrieved employee. (3) There was no evidence of any management prejudice toward the union steward. (4) The same steward had been disciplined twice before during that year under this company's progressive-discipline plan.[22]

The only thing that saved another union president from having his discharge upheld by an arbitrator was his 12 years of service with the company and his good record during that time. However, his reinstatement was nevertheless without any back-pay award. The events leading to his discharge for insubordination, which was claimed discriminatory by the union, consisted of his changing the feeds and speeds on his machine in order to obtain a faster production cycle. This occurred after all employees had been warned not to change the posted speeds and feeds. The employer had a right, subject to the grievance procedure, to establish what it deemed the proper feeds, speeds, and cycles in order to preserve its machines and tools. Significant in the decision was the absence of any evidence that the union president had been disciplined more severely than other employees for the same offense or because of his union activities.[23]

A total reversal of a management discharge action resulted after an employer was held not justified in discharging an individual as allegedly guilty of (1) *deliberate* scattering and misplacing of essential parts required to reactivate certain production machinery, (2) displaying an attitude of insubordination in refusing to obey his foreman's order directing him to attempt to get the machinery back in operation, (3) attempting to create unrest among several other employees, and (4) a generally unsatisfactory approach toward members of the employer's staff.

Dealing with each of these management complaints against the grievant, the arbitrator disposed of them in the following manner: First, granting that the employee did not keep his parts neatly assembled and readily accessible, the evidence did not support a finding that the employee had *deliberately* or *willfully* scattered or misplaced the parts. The most that could be held against him was that he might be considered guilty of "bad housekeeping" (the company had claimed it was deliberate). Second, the employee had been suspended for refusing to obey his foreman's order. Therefore, the arbitrator declined to accept as evidence to support the discharge action the existence of facts and circumstances for which this other disciplinary penalty had previously been invoked. Third, the arbitrator felt he gained valuable insights into the employer's motivation when the accused was called more "vigilant" than the previous shop chairman. This was management's claim about this employee, who had recently been elected the chairman of the union shop committee, filing a grievance protesting the employer's shifting of employees in alleged violation of the contract. Without in any way implying that the employee's suspension was retaliatory, the arbiter believed it could not be totally dismissed from consideration that the company representatives were manifestly perturbed by the new shop committeeman's unwillingness "to leave things as they were." Fourth, the employer's representatives were not at all pleased with the employee's election to union office, and this attitude was evidenced by his foreman, who had threatened to "get rid of" him. In this context it is certainly understandable that discharge, the ultimate penalty, could not be sustained merely because an employee who was a representative of the union "stood up" for other employees' rights.

The arbiter was compelled to make such an award unless the union representative's defiance had resulted in willful disobedience or a disregard for rules and regulations – or perhaps created such a disruptive influence that shop morale would be substantially affected. None of these elements were present in this case.

The foreman, because of his close relationship with the workers and their problems, feels a closeness and kinship with the workers which most other management representatives do not share. As a member of management, and as their spokesman and advocate, he may sometimes find himself in conflict with his personal feelings toward the issue, as opposed to a management position he must endorse. The steward faces similar problems. His close association with the employees subjects him to certain group pressures and thinking to which he as an individual and an employee may not subscribe. All of these elements are present when these two advocates come together. Each has a job to do and should be performing it in the manner which best serves the interests of his institution as well as the organization as a whole. To accomplish their joint and mutual purpose effectively, each must treat the other with the respect due his office. Obviously, the company and the union have met on equal terms and adopted a contract recognizing each other's rights. Now each has its dignity to uphold. Organizations and corporations can act only through agents and representatives. To the extent each treats the other with respect, the job of resolving their joint problems will be enhanced.

Now it is probably advisable to examine the other side of this coin – that is, where management's conduct was such as to have contributed to emotional eruptions in a dispute. Typical of such situations was one involving a construction company and the Teamsters. In this dispute, the owner assigned his brother to operate a truck, although he carried a classification as a laborer. When challenged by the union steward about the propriety of this assignment, a heated conversation resulted which was discussed by the arbitrator in his published decision:

> [The employer] admittedly violated the Collective Agreement when he permitted his brother, who was classified as a laborer, to operate a truck. The fact that this would help get the job done does not excuse the violation, for the Contract cannot be set aside to suit the convenience of one of the

Parties. X, as Union Steward, had a right, indeed a duty, to call this violation to the attention of the employer and to make known the union's objection. [Employer's] response that no one was going to tell him who he would put on a truck was contrary to the obligation he had agreed to under the Contract to assign only truckers to drive trucks, and it overlooked the basic fact that when he signed the Collective Bargaining Agreement he limited his freedom to run his business as he might from moment to moment choose.

Furthermore, collective bargaining requires each party to treat the other with respect. An employer had no more right to submit a union steward to verbal abuse for presenting a grievance in good faith than a steward has to submit a foreman or others in management to verbal abuse for issuing orders in good faith. Nothing X did can excuse, much less justify, the language of [the employer].[24]

The result of this dispute was that the employer discharged the steward for too vigorously arguing the union's position. The end result of the arbiter's decision was that the steward was reinstated with partial back pay since "five weeks of work and earnings have been lost, with both the employer and the union steward sharing responsibility for the claim of events which led to this loss."

The permanent arbitrator under an agreement with International Harvester and the UAW handled a dispute where management had discharged a union steward for refusal to obey a foreman's order that he discontinue working on a grievance. Another employee, a probationer, had been discharged, and the steward was in the process of working up a valid grievance. The reaction of the steward to the foreman's order was calm, dignified, and respectful but also final in the position that he had a right as a union representative to continue his pursuit of these legitimate union activities permitted by the agreement.

Article VI, Section 8(a) stated:

Sec. 8. The recognized stewards and grievance committeemen should be afforded such time off by the company during their regularly scheduled working hours as may be required for the performance of the following functions within the works:

(a). A steward while making an investigation of a grievance in Step 1 of the grievance procedure within his designated area, provided he informs his supervisor of the nature of the grievance and-or the identity of the aggrieved employee before making such investigation.

In his opinion, the arbitrator stated:

There is a clear distinction between the case of a supervisor telling an employee to go back to his position, and a supervisor telling the union to

stop investigating a grievance. The company and the union have met on
equal terms and adopted a contract recognizing each other's rights each
has its dignity to uphold. Organizations and corporations can act only
through agents and representatives. When the duly authorized representative of the company told the duly authorized representative of the union
to stop investigating a grievance, it was the company issuing orders to the
union. If [supervisor] had been right, it would have been [the steward's]
duty as an employee to go back to his job. But [supervisor] was wrong . . .
and it was [steward's] duty, speaking as the representative of the union,
to insist firmly but respectfully upon the union's rights.

The company argues that with such a principle supervisors will never
dare issue orders to union representatives, and discipline will be gone. That
is a slightly exaggerated view. The rule of military law referred to above
has produced no such result in the army. But it has had the effect of causing
officers to learn the rules so as to avoid the giving of orders that can be
declined with impunity. If this decision has that effect upon supervisors,
causing them to study the contract and be sure before they act, and causes
them to refrain from arrogating to themselves the power to decide for the
Steward whether grounds for a grievance exist, no unfortunate result need
be anticipated. The company has express protection in the contract against
abuse of the privilege of union representatives, in that it can refuse pay to
them.[25]

As the arbitrator went on to say, the company was insisting on a
strict adherence by the union to the grievance machinery but asking the
arbitrator to do what amounted to sustaining a foreman in denying the
union access to it. Therefore, the arbiter sustained the union's grievance,
setting aside the discharge action and making the employee whole for all
wages lost.

Employees crossing a picket line and going to work during a strike
were the reason for a problem between an employer and the union
representing its employees. During the negotiations leading to the
resolution of this strike and a new agreement, the parties had entered
a "termination of strike agreement" which read as follows:

Employees returned hereunder shall be restored to service to full roster
seniority. The company and the union and the employees of the company
covered by this agreement shall cooperate fully to restore the company's
normal operations as rapidly as possible. In the furtherance of such objective, the parties agree that neither the company nor the union shall engage
in any reprisals or retaliation, legal or otherwise, or take any vindictive actions whatsoever against the other or against any of such employees as a
result of or in connection with the strike against the company by the
BRC.

Despite this agreement between the parties, subsequent to the return to work, a union officer preferred charges in the union against those union employees who went to work across the picket line during the strike. For this action the employer imposed a disciplinary suspension. Conceding that in taking retaliatory measures against any of its members for refusing to participate in the strike, the union was in violation of the termination of the strike agreement, this finding was not determinative or dispositive of the issue of discipline in this case. Because the officer was acting as an agent of the union in preferring the charges against the union members, his actions could not be said to be related to his work performance or his employment status. Whatever remedy the company had with respect to its asserted violations of the provisions of the strike-termination agreement would have been against the union, not against an individual in his employment status. The union official was acting as an agent of the union engaged in strictly an intra-union action. For these reasons, the arbitrator was constrained to hold there was no basis for the imposition of discipline against the union official.[26]

Always prominent is the complicated question of the degree of disciplinary authority the company may exercise over employees who also hold union office and are functioning in that capacity. Management always worries that to the degree its authority is not recognized, the employee's role as a union official may be used as a shield in cases of irresponsible conduct which fall outside the scope of proper union duties. On the other hand, the union always worries that to the degree the company's authority is recognized, the union representative's status as an employee may be used by the company as an excuse for handcuffing him in the pursuit of his union duties. No easy formulas present themselves that will avoid the dilemma coming from this dual role. As a union representative, the individual is on an equal level with management representatives in his relationships with the company. As an employee, he is subject to the company's rules and discipline. It would be very easy to state that a union official is immune to discipline when he is acting within the recognized purview of his union activities but still subjects himself to discipline when he exceeds such boundaries. Saying this is easy, but making the judgment whether he is inside or outside the boundaries of legitimate activities is the question. The answer is often elusive.

Commenting on this problem, one arbitrator put it this way:

> The question answered of management is that in dealing with the rights of union representatives, as in any other contractual question, management

has the right to make the initial decision and if the union representative does not like that decision, he should, nevertheless, obey it and file a grievance. But this is the ultimate implicator of this answer. It necessarily assumed that if the union representative disagrees with management's interpretation of his rights and disobeys a management order to cease certain activities, he may be suspended or discharged. An unscrupulous management, then, could destroy a union and prevent any serious attempt to enforce the agreement, merely by ordering union representatives to stop performing their duties, and – if they refused to obey – suspending or discharging them. Subsequent arbitration awards, which found for the union as to the rights of its representatives should have obeyed the order and filed grievances, would only serve to emphasize the futility of the union position. The question is not whether this company would dream of attempting such a thing. The question is whether the arbitrator could properly adopt an interpretation of "good cause" which would make such an attempt possible.

Thus posed, of course, the issue is unrealistic – not an example of the dangers of pushing a sound principle to ridiculous extremes. When the union representatives are clearly right in what they are trying to do, management concedes that they should not be required to obey a "cease and desist" order or become subject to suspension or discharge. But the reverse, management says, is likewise true. When a union representative is clearly wrong, he should be subject to discipline; else his status as a steward or committeeman would in effect, give him carte blanche to run wild in the plant.[27]

This arbitrator went on to point out that at first blush the development of such a management thesis does seem to provide a sound rule to this dilemma, which is created by the union official's dual role. But this presents a latent difficulty. Who was to decide when the union representative was "clearly" right or "clearly" wrong? An arbitrator may act after the event, but what happened in the meantime? What is the position of a union representative who *sincerely* believes that he is clearly right, even though the arbitrator later finds that he was clearly wrong? In determining its proper course of action whether to cease and desist as ordered, at the possible sacrifice of rights of employees to representation, or to obey and run the risk of a penalty, is he required to decide not only what his rights are but also whether those rights are clear under the agreement? And is he properly subject to discipline if he interprets the agreement with a clarity, which is the arbitrator's subsequent judgment, that is not there?

Admitting that he would be the last to assert that he had reached a satisfactory answer to these questions, which could fairly and properly solve all of the problems which might arise, the arbiter was led to the conclusion that a sound decision had to give weight to three factors:

1. The good faith of the union representative in asserting his belief that he was acting in accordance with his rights under the agreement;
2. The existence somewhere in the agreement or in the practices in the plant of a reasonable grounds for that belief to be held by the union representative;
3. The nature of the right he is asserting – whether it is a right to represent employees or a collateral right less directly related to the union's principal and essential function.

In reviewing these factors as they applied to the case, the arbitrator ruled that the discharge of the union official was not for "just cause" under the contract.

In many factories, responsible union officials are sensitive to the need for reasonable grievance adjudication and the necessity to remove all internal roadblocks which cause friction or failures. In far too many labor-management situations, internal union politics, manifested in various forms, interferes with or prevents the orderly and responsible settlement of grievance disputes. But irrespective of the particular bent of union officials, the sophisticated management representative recognizes that the union is basically a political organization with political motivations. Its needs are many and varied but can usually be categorized into one or more of four factors. First, to perpetuate itself, it must always be seeking "more" for its members – additional wages, improved benefits, better working conditions, fewer hours but without reduced income, greater voice in how the plant is run, and a host of others. Second, it must constantly be striving to increase its membership since dues from employees constitute its lifeblood; it must therefore invariably contest any management effort to mechanize or make technological changes which produce a need for fewer workers. Third, it must always be alert to ways to improve its economic status, and this may be accomplished in a variety of ways. It commonly seeks company payment of union time for grievance processing and investigations and for a myriad of other union activities attendant to administering the labor agreement. By so doing, it acts to reduce the drain on its economic resources. Fourth, it must always be "competitive." The needs and desires of its membership must be met – or at least the members must be of the opinion that the union is doing everything in its power to satisfy those needs. Unless this is happening – and since other unions are constantly coming along and suggesting to organized workers that they may be able to represent them more effectively than the incumbent organization – the union may suffer a loss in its competition with others for the workers loyalty. All of these factors are ever present in the minds of the union's representatives, and they should be as well known and understood by the management's representatives. It is factors such as these which add to the complexity of situations arising out of the union officials' dual-capacity conduct.

Chapter 2

Union Activities on Company Time and Property

It should be remembered that the parties to a labor agreement generally intend to establish by the grievance machinery a procedure which will fulfill two basic objectives: (1) to facilitate the investigation and resolution of problems and grievances in a peaceful manner and (2) to do this in a fashion which will interfere as little as possible with the orderly and efficient operation of the business. These two basic objectives should be balanced in meeting any situation which develops the grievance procedure. Procedures of this sort require mutual consideration, good faith, tolerance, and cooperation if they are to be successful. These are the implied obligations lying at the back of every grievance procedure which are customarily acknowledged by sophisticated and responsible adversaries from each party.

In the typical contract, whenever an employee has or claims to have a complaint, he and or his union steward present it first to the foreman. If the answer of the foreman does not settle the complaint, it is formalized and appealed. At this first step, the steward of the department and the employee devote time to the preparation of the complaint to be presented to the foreman with the hope that the grievance of the employee will be settled equitably. Sometimes these matters take a little time and occasionally more time than management would like.

In any such circumstances, the company has a right to expect some reasonable form of procedure in the handling of grievances. It should be understood, however, that the procedure for handling and discussing, and the conditions surrounding the adjustment process, must be flexible enough not to impair the underlying purpose of the grievance machinery. In this regard, both parties have essential needs which must be satisfied.

An agreement between Brown & Sharpe Manufacturing and the International Association of Machinists did not clearly cover the question of the company's right to refuse to permit a representative of the union to handle union business during working hours, but on the employee's own time, off company property. It was clear, however, that the contract contemplated that union officers would be permitted some time to attend to union business since another provision of the agreement provided that such time would be counted as time worked for purposes of computing overtime. Still another provision of the contract allowed that leaves of absence for employees delegated as official union representatives for an initial period not to exceed three months, with consideration for leaves of longer periods.

The company contended that in the interests of good management it must have the right to refuse permission to an employee to be absent from the plant during working hours to conduct personal business. Therefore, as a special case arising under this general proposition, they contended they had the right to refuse an employee who was a union official permission to leave the plant on union business or to stay away from the plant to carry on union business.

The union pointed out that under the agreement reports on unadjusted grievances to the general grievances committee had to be made "outside of scheduled working hours." Since it was necessary for this union official to pass upon such grievances and to pursue other union duties, the company did not have an absolute right to refuse to permit the representative to handle this type of necessary union business off the company premises but during working hours.

The essence of the final arbitral decision:

> It is the opinion of the undersigned that, if union business caused an employee to take off so much time as to destroy his usefulness as a productive employee, the employee should be obliged to take recourse to the leave of absence provision. Therefore, it is within the company's rights, under such circumstances, to refuse to permit employee representatives to go off company premises where this occurs excessively to handle necessary union business during working hours or for any other reason.[1]

Under another agreement, by her own admission, a local union official erased any question as to her guilt that she was carrying on her union activities during working hours. The union contended that her activity would not interfere with the production of the plant. However, the arbitrator was of the opinion that such conduct, including calling employees scabs, did interfere with the production of the plant. Here, the arbitrator was called upon to decide whether the rights of the employee under the contract had been violated.[2]

Arbitrator Harold M. Gilden was faced with a contract which required the continuance of "local working conditions agreed to by local collective bargaining" and a local practice of management permitting the distribution of union literature during nonworking time. The union contended that the practice was established by bargaining because a company plant superintendent had once stated in a bargaining session that he had no objection to the practice. There was no evidence that at any subsequent time the parties had discussed the conditions or stipulations of such an agreement or settled definitely upon its purpose. Since the company denied the existence of this agreement, the union was required to furnish clear and convincing proof of its existence, a circumstance it failed to meet. In view of these factors, the arbitrator held that the procedures invoked were not sufficiently definite, specific, or precise to prove a joint agreement resulting from collective bargaining which would permit the distribution of the union literature on plant premises.

He concluded that under the wording of the above-quoted provision, working conditions had to be agreed to by local collective bargaining in order to come within its scope. For that reason, the arbitrator did not give consideration to the argument that the union's right to distribute the literature was an established custom and an integral part of the plant's working conditions. However, similarly, the contractural limitations on the arbitrator's authority precluded him from deciding whether the company's denial of the right to distribute literature unlawfully deprived the union of its constitutional guarantees. Unanswered, therefore, was the question whether the company's action contravened the policy of the National Labor Relations Board. Whether the union would have received a different decision from that tribunal was a question beyond this arbitration hearing.[3]

When one arbitrator was dealing with an issue involving a no-distribution ruling he turned to *Webster's New International Dictionary* for the definition of these terms. Therein, he found *distribution* defined as "an apportionment among several or many." This definition proved to be quite significant in this dispute since a plant rule in question was obviously not designed to cover this type of incident–the discharge of an employee–union member for alleged repeated violations of a plant rule prohibiting distribution of union or other literature on company time and property. The rule stated, "There shall be no distribution or posting by employees or by the union of notices, pamphlets, advertisements, political matter or other literature of any kind on company property other than as provided in this Article."

The type referred to in "other than as provided in this Article" dealt with bulletin-board notices for official union positions. One of the employee's alleged violations of this rule consisted of handing to a fellow union steward one copy of a small leaflet urging the picketing of Polytechnic High School on the occasion of a speech there by a well-known American exponent of Nazi-Fascist doctrines. It was admitted by the company that no time loss resulted from this transmittal and that the employee was not observed passing material to any other employees. His second offense consisted of handing out to workers coming on the shift union leaflets attacking the company's policy with respect to returning veterans. This incident occurred on company property but before the commencement of the shift. His third offense consisted of distributing to union members on company time a number of union-dues cards. The arbitrator viewed the first two offenses as nonviolative of the rule on no distribution, but the company was well within its rights in reprimanding the employee for the third offense. The arbitrator's comments on this matter are particularly relevant and well grounded in logic and practical labor-relations administration, and are related to the employee's first alleged violation:

> Unauthorized distribution rules are usually adopted to avoid three general situations: (1) waste of company time caused by the passing out and reading of the material; (2) littering of company premises with discarded leaflets, pamphlets, etc.; and (3) tensions and bickering incited by the controversial nature of the distributed material. Obviously, _____'s action resulted in none of these undesirable situations. If he was, in fact, guilty of unauthorized distribution on this occasion, then any employee who so much as hands a written invitation to attend a party to another employee on company time must necessarily be guilty of the same offense. So construed, the unauthorized distribution rule would be reduced to an absurdity and could in no event be consistently enforced.[4]

The records and minutes of contract negotiations may also be pertinent in deciding a dispute. It is not uncommon for the union to attempt to obtain through the grievance procedure what it failed to obtain in collective bargaining. When this occurs, management is understandably disturbed and generally considers the union to be operating in bad faith. Naturally, if either party attempts to achieve an objective through formal contract negotiations, exchanges proposals, and engages in discussions on an issue but fails to achieve its objective, it should be foreclosed from endeavoring to obtain this goal during the term of that agreement. Unfortunately, management occasionally engages in this kind of illicit and self-serving activity. Claiming a right under its managements-rights clause, an employer instituted unilaterally a practice of requiring union stewards to report to their work stations and obtain passes from their foremen before each individual employee contract for grievance business.

Exploring all of the pertinent factors of the case, the arbitrator inquired into and was fully apprised of the relevance of prior bargaining discussions on this point. The contract language read, in Article 4, Section 2, paragraph (b): "Union representatives report when: Each representative of the union shall report to his regular place of work in accordance with the provisions of this Article, shall remain there during working hours, unless permission of his supervisor not to so report has been given."

The union argued that a new management had been transferred from another facility into this location and was desiring greater control over the grievance machinery and the grievance handler. To achieve this goal, the new management had ordered union representatives to report to their supervisors after each employee contact. The union contended that this unilateral action was contrary to a past practice which had allowed the union representative multiple employee contacts.

The arbitrator found that that the above-cited contractual provision was silent on this matter. However, the provision had not always been silent. In the agreement preceding this one, the wording of Article 4, Section 2(b) read as follows: "Union representatives report when: Each representative of the union shall report to his regular place of work: (1) at the commencement of his regular shift, (2) after any lunch period, and (3) *immediately upon completion of any duties as a union representative*" (emphasis supplied).

The contractual requirement of subparagraph 3 was removed from this contract effective with the date of the new agreement. From that date until approximately four years later, the record showed that multiple contacts by stewards and chief stewards were generally permitted. The company's principal contention was that the reinstatement of what in effect was requirement 3 was a legitimate exercise of managerial discretion. The company interpreted its management-prerogatives clause to mean that that management had a free hand to operate the plant except as its rights were clearly restricted by the terms of the agreement or some statute. Deciding that the company was in violation of Article 4 by requiring stewards and chief stewards to obtain separate passes for each contact made for union duties, the arbitrator noted:

> The parties must have had some motivation in taking the affirmative action which they did in 1958 in deleting the third requirement from Article 4, Section 2 (b). The arbitrator must assume that it was the mutual intent of the parties to eliminate this requirement.
> In light of the 1956 change of contract language and the subsequent practice of multiple contracts by stewards until 1962, the arbitrator is of the

opinion that the requirement #3 cannot be reinstated unilaterally. It seems to the arbitrator that the appropriate method of reinstating requirement #3 would be through contract negotiations. Otherwise, it would be possible to unilaterally impose as plant rules specific conditions or requirements which had been deleted from the contract through mutual agreement of the parties in negotiations.[5]

Presumably the new management team which instituted this change did so either without knowledge of the prior negotiation experience and its connection or with knowledge of it but in a genuine belief that such right was retained under their management clause. Irrespective of which situation applied, clearly it would have been advisable for management to have given greater weight to the contract negotiations records. Whenever the question arises whether language changes have occurred or the prior intent of the parties reformed, management representative should turn to the negotiations records or to participating individuals to fill this void. The research should be in pursuit of the following types of information:

1. Is there a *new* or *changed* contract provision on the grieved matter?

2. If a *new* provision exists, which party proposed the language and what were the reasons for them seeking the change? In this regard, which party's language was eventually adopted?

3. If the contractual provision had been *changed* from that which appeared in the prior contract, who proposed the change and what were their reasons? In this regard, which party's proposal was finally adopted?

4. Were minutes of the negotiation meetings kept and what do those minutes reveal regarding the discussions between the parties on the provision in dispute, irrespective of whether it is a new, a change, or an unchanged clause?

5. Who represented management in these negotiations and was present during discussions on the relevant provisions? Is that individual available and able to supply credible accounts of what the parties intended?

6. Did the union attempt to insert language in the contract to cover an uncovered subject but fail to accomplish it?

Applying some of these questions to actual cases may supply a better insight into the role and significance of prior bargaining sessions to current disputes between the parties.

Even where the contract provisions are liberal in their allowance of time for company-paid union business, some reasonable limitations may be imposed to control abuse of such time. In one of those infrequent cases where management files a grievance, a company submitted one to the union in the form of a letter to the employee, who was also the union president, warning him that disciplinary action would ensue if he did not spend more of his time on work for the employer instead of union business. This occurred under a contract which was more generous in its company-paid time for union business than the average agreement. A company review of the employee's work records revealed that he had not performed his occupational duties for a period of at least six months except on six days, and then only for a period of approximately two hours or less during each day. In this case, it was relevant that the union had proposed during negotiations that the company provide a 40-hour week for the union president to conduct his union affairs, provided only that he remain in the plant during the hours for which he would be paid. However, this proposal was rejected by the company, and no such provision appeared in the agreement. After the contract was signed, it was brought to the attention of the union president that he was spending little, if any time, on his job as a workman. In the discussion which followed the company went so far as stating that it would not object to the president's spending a reasonable time on union business, suggesting that he be allowed two hours a day for this purpose. The union official contended that this time would be grossly inadequate.

It was the arbitrator's judgment that despite the provisions in the agreement respecting the right of union officials to a sufficient time without loss of pay to handle grievances, there was nothing in the agreement which indicated that such union representatives might spend all or a greater portion of their time during working hours on such activities. He further observed that it was customary in many plants which require the services of a full-time union agent to have such officials on the union's payroll. In fact, having union officials on the company's payroll – particularly where this type of thing occurred along with other favors which were furnished at company expense – could conceivably be deemed evidence of domination by the company and might suggest the possibility of an unfair-practice charge under Section 8(a)(2) of the Labor Management Relations Act. It was the arbiter's conclusion that the company's letter in question was not coercive or in violation of the agreement and did not deny the union's president any of the rights granted to him by the expressed terms of the agreement.[6]

Occasionally the labor agreement may provide that union officials must conduct their union business *outside* working hours. Such was the case where an employer issued a disciplinary verbal reprimand to a union steward for processing grievances on two occasions after the steward clocked in for work early and conducted his union business before going to work. On each occasion, as a result of handling this union business, he reported to his work station approximately one minute late. The agreement here provided in Article 4: "Stewards shall discharge their duties, as far as possible, outside working hours, and in any event in such manner as to interfere as little as possible in the operation of the plant. In the event it becomes necessary for a steward to leave his work station, for the purpose of discharging his duties, he shall first notify his immediate supervisor and receive permission to leave his work station. Such permission, consistent with production requirements, shall not be unreasonably withheld. The steward shall punch out immediately upon departure from his work station and punch in on his return."

The company's contentions were two. First, the employee twice violated company rules when he failed to report timely to his work station. Second, he failed to abide with Article 4 when he conducted union business after punching in to work and continued to pursue such activities after the time to start work. I must concur with the arbitrator who decided this issue that the company's interpretation of the contractual provision took an unreasonably strict view of the ground rules for the conduct of union stewards. The contract language contained no prohibition on the employee punching in prior to his working hours and using this time to process grievances. Clearly, he was on his own time and not on company time, and the agreement did not restrict his union activities during such periods.

As a matter of fact, he was operating in precise accord with the agreement in conducting his business outside working hours – and in a fashion which interfered as little as possible with the normal functions of the plant. Naturally, this second ingredient of not interfering with production is essential for the union representatives' conduct to be viewed as completely proper.[7]

Moving from this case to one at the other end of the scale, a gross example of interference was present in the next situation. A shop steward under an agreement between Dwight Manufacturing Co. and the Textile Workers Union of America left his work station taking six or seven other employees with him during working hours. They were wending their way toward a supervisor's office in connection with a grievance when they met another supervisor. Since neither the head supervisor nor his assistant was available, this other supervisor settled the grievance then and there, and the men went back to work. The company subsequently reprimanded the steward for taking the men off the job to discuss a grievance without having received prior permission or making prior arrangements. The steward appealed this action.

The arbitrator's opinion was short and succinct: "Obviously this grievance is without merit. When the number of employees involved in a grievance is so great that taking them off the job would interfere with production and upset morale and discipline, the shop steward should see the overseer or the Second Hand, and endeavor to make arrangements for the first step in the Grievance machinery. Cooperation on the part of the supervisory force and the shop stewards is necessary in order to effect as prompt a settlement as possible without unnecessary interruptions of work."[8]

This is precisely the kind of difficulty the grievance procedure has been designed to prevent. Few matters can be considered as sufficiently urgent to justify six or seven employees leaving their work stations without permission and prior arrangements to avoid interruption of production to process a complaint.

An interesting issue developed under a contract which (1) required employees to work the scheduled work days surrounding a holiday to qualify for holiday pay but (2) further provided that if the employee was absent due to union business, such days would be considered as not scheduled. On December 30, a short time before the start of the last shift, the union delivered by hand a letter to the company requesting it to "please excuse all union members for union business from working overtime and working December 31 and January 1." For a number of reasons, the company was unable to take any action on the union's request, and a large number of employees did not report for work on these dates. On January 1 at 11:12 A.M., the union by a telegram to the company requested, "Please extend the leave of absence of all members of the union for January 2." A large number of employees did not report for work on that date.

The grievance and subsequent arbitration resulted from the employer's declining to pay holiday pay to those employees who were scheduled to work and because of the union's request, did not work the shifts surrounding the holiday. Under the contract language mentioned above, the union contended that the company was obligated to excuse "all" union members. Denying the union's claim, the arbitrator commented:

> A practical reading of the clause would make it appear reasonable that what the parties intended was to excuse upon request, employees such as union officers, shop stewards and even some lay members who might actually be engaged in certified union business. By so specifying each employee, the contract requirement, though it refers to employee in the singular, would have been complied with.
>
> To accept the union's interpretation of this clause would be tantamount

to ceding to the union control of plant operations on shifts surrounding the holiday, a situation likewise obviously not intended by the parties.

In the past, when the union desired to have certain employees excused from working the shifts surrounding a holiday, its request to the employer would specify the names of the employees so sought to be excused. The employer, upon granting such request, was then in a position to adjust its plant operations so as to continue work with a reduced force. Here, however, the request was a blanket one for all employees, which, if acceded to, would have required a plant-wide shutdown.[9]

This is another example of an abuse of union discretion. Clearly, no employer in possession of his senses would negotiate a contract provision which enabled the union legitimately, without management recourse, to shut down the company's operations every time a holiday occurred. Under the same type of illogical premise, a union might conceivably employ such a contract clause to allow the union to find justification for excusing its members absent on days surrounding a holiday for reasons other than union business. If enabled to do so, it would render the qualifying-day requirement for holiday pay a useless provision of the agreement.

Sometimes to ensure the continuation of plant operations, it is understood that the union representative will notify his foreman before leaving his work station and before embarking on union business on company paid time. Normally this can be accomplished without any inconvenience to anyone. To conclude that this control would offend the principle of grievance handling is clearly without merit.

The typical attitudes which manifest themselves over such issues result from the implications each party sees from its vantage point. The management is concerned lest the union representative, given an inch, will take a mile, that he might roam the plant at will, and that the shop might become a forum for an interminable debating society over every incipient grievance. The union envisions its union representative so hobbled in his movements that to all intents and purposes he will be unable to perform the union's functions adequately, and thereby the employees will be disenfranchised. It is perhaps too dramatic to accept either premise as entirely valid, but the intensity of the attitude of each party certainly reflects the need for equitable mechanics for governing the union representative's function. For this reason, it is well to examine how certain arbitrators have decided questions of what latitude should be allowed union representatives and what conduct might constitute interruptions of operations.

In a dispute between Armstrong Cork Co. and the Textile Workers Union, the company denied the union the right to bring in an international staff man to make a time study to determine the adequacy of new production standards. The relevant contractual clauses read:

Section 8.6:

The company recognizes that some grievances by their very nature require investigation on the job; and it, therefore, agrees that it will issue within reason special temporary passes to any employee member or members of the Grievance Committee to permit him or them to enter specified areas of the plant for the purpose of adjusting or making an investigation of such grievances as may arise, under the terms of this Agreement. Such member or members of the Grievance Committee shall contact the Foreman or Department Head immediately upon entering the department advise him of the purpose of the visit.

Any representative of the Union, not an employee of the Company, shall be permitted to enter the plant by first calling upon and arranging with the Plant Manager or the Assistant Plant Manager or the designated alternate, prior to entering.

It is mutually agreed that such visits shall be so conducted as not to interfere with employees engaged in work and shall be confined to the departments of the plant in the specific grievance.[10]

The company contended that as a matter of past practice there had been numerous prior discussions between the company and union representatives about disputed time standards, and on no occasion was an international staff man brought in or had the union made such a request. On this point, the arbitrator ruled that (1) in all past cases the parties had been able to work out a settlement on the disputed standards, and (2) even more important, it was an established premise in labor arbitration that where precedent and the contract point in opposite directions, the contract remained the governing consideration (not all arbiters would accord with this philosophy on past practice). He viewed the language as clear and unequivocal. In finding for the union, the arbitrator made these observations:

The Company's contention that to allow the International Staff man to make a time-study of the operations would disrupt the work of the various employees, is without merit. There is no foundation, in either logic or experience, for the argument – implicitly espoused by the Company – that an Industrial Engineer employed by the Company or by an outside consulting firm would not disrupt work while the same type of time study made by the International Staff man would generate disruption. . . . And the grievance procedure clearly and unequivocally gives the Union the right to bring in an International Staff man (or "any representative of the Union, not an employee of the Company") for the purpose of investigating a grievance.

The only question remaining therefore, is whether "grievance investigation" encompasses the right of an international Staff man to make a time
study of disputes standards. To that question we now turn.

Section 8.6 states: "The Company recognizes that some grievances by
their very nature may require *investigation on the job.*" This clearly implies
that, in the case of disputed incentive standards, time studies by an International Staff man are permissive. For how else can the Staff man determine accurately whether the standards are proper or not.

Now, in this matter it is evident that an "outside" union representative was involved rather than an "inside" one. But the issue still turned
around a company claim that disruption of operations would result from
this form of grievance investigation during working hours. It was the
kind of circumstance which plainly justifies involvement of union
representatives in grievance investigation while employees are working,
without the attendant result that productive operations are disrupted or
interfered with.

But what of the situation where such an interference or interruption
may be brought about by the grievance handling during working hours?
The Oliver Corporation and the United Farm Equipment and Metal
Workers had a dispute over a company transfer of a union representative
to another job. The issue was whether this individual's rights under Section 28 of the contract had been violated. The contract read: "Section
28 – Any local union representative after reporting to his supervisor,
who will make arrangements for his relief if necessary, will be permitted,
after stamping his time card out, can leave his work for the purpose of
handling grievances.... The union representative shall return to his
work as quickly as possible and shall stamp his time card in upon so doing."

It was agreed that the company had the right to transfer within the
given job classifications. The union was not concerned with the right of
transfer as such but whether this particular transfer was in violation of
the employee's rights as a union representative. The evidence showed
that on every occasion in the past when the union official had asked for
permission to leave the job, it had been granted. Nor in the past had
anyone been placed on her job when she was absent. However, the contractual requirement under Section 28 was for relief "if necessary," and
this provision did not set up the employee as the judge of the necessity.
The arbiter held that Section 28 was a guarantee that the union
representative had the right to leave the job, but it gave no other right,
and he could not add such a right to this section.

The company's motivation was based solely on the fact that the union official was required to be away from her work frequently for the union business, while her old job was such that it needed constant attendance. The transfer was not intended to reduce her opportunities to go on union business. It was just that her absence from the new job to attend to union business was less troublesome to the maintenance and continuance of the company's operation.[11]

Now let's look at a contract clause which appears clear and unambiguous on its face but if literally administered could result in a serious interference with management's operations. The contract here centered on an employer-established rule prohibiting the processing of grievances in a stockroom. The relevant contract provision stated: "Section 23 – When any aggrieved employee is desirous of having his district steward called to his job to discuss his grievance, a request for the district steward will be made by such employee to his foreman and the district steward shall immediately be sent for by the foreman."

During the term of the agreement, the company advised the union that the stockroom was no longer to be used for processing grievances. The company argued the area in the stockroom customarily used by the union was on the main aisle, around which there was considerable activity, and that processing of grievances at this location seriously interfered with work in the stockroom. However, the employer did not preclude the union from conducting this activity outside the stockroom.

The union contended that management's order violated the provision and that based on past practice, grievances had been written and processed in the stockroom. The arbitrator's findings in this case show him particularly astute and sensitive to the needs of both parties, and his award not only does no injury to either party but facilitates and services their respective needs:

> It can scarcely be argued, however, that the language of Section 23 was intended to give employees a vested right to discuss their grievances in one particular physical location in the plant. So long as an employee's right to call his steward for consultation while on the job is protected, he has no cause for complaint.... His right to discuss his grievance with (union officials) was limited in no material respect by the order to do so outside the stockroom, and there can be little doubt that his objective was based upon other considerations.

It is plain to see that Section 23 permitted an aggrieved employee to call his district steward "to his job."

As wisely observed by the arbitrator, the language of Section 23 had to be read not in a sense of literalness but with a view to effectuating its basic intent. The purpose of the provision is clear: to permit an employee to avail himself of the counsel of his union representative without having to leave the general area of his work. It may be observed that this provision appears to have been drafted with the company's interests as well as the union's in mind, for it ensures among other things that employees will not have to go wandering about the plant in search of their union representative.[12]

Where a labor agreement set forth the regular hours of work as "7 A.M. to 3:30 P.M. with ½ hour for lunch between 12 noon and 12:30 P.M." employees who quit their work before 3:30 P.M. for purposes of attending a union meeting were held in violation of the contract. The union contended that under past practice they had the right to hold shop meetings during working hours, but failed to submit any evidence that such an accepted past practice existed. On the contrary, the evidence established that on past occasions when the union called shop meetings during working hours, the company had objected.[13]

It is very doubtful that any expert or qualified authority in the field of labor relations would deny that a "union-shop" arrangement tends to strengthen and enhance the effectiveness of virtually every union. Further, such qualified practitioners would agree that the absence or loss of a union-shop clause will tend to weaken the union in many ways, some obvious and others subtle. Even President Kennedy spoke in defense of a recommendation by a specially appointed board in a major aerospace dispute when a union shop was advocated by the board. It is plain that there is every indication of the high value placed on the union shop by all organized trade unions.

Sears, Roebuck and the Retail Clerks International Association had a labor agreement in one location that provided for a union-steward system. As it operated under this contract, the steward system was designed and developed as a substitute for a conventional union-shop clause. Somehow, in its operation it apparently had approximately the same effect as the union-shop clause. During the term of the agreement and without the consent of the union, the company unilaterally changed the steward system, resulting in a union contention that this action, for all intents and purposes, served to demolish the steward system. If it did not render it completely inoperative, it caused it to be substantially ineffective. The company argued that its action did not abolish the steward system but only modified it to the extent that company management and the department-store-association executives no longer participated.

With regard to this contention, the arbitrator found that the steward system was vitiated by the withdrawal of top management from active participation and consequently that the union was damaged by the company's unilateral change in the steward system in violation of the existing contract. Accordingly, he ruled the union was entitled to an award of damages to compensate it for the loss of membership dues, fees, and related revenues.[14]

Union activity which interrupts management's operations may consist of union representatives leaving the plant to conduct union business off work premises. Absences of this nature from the employee's work station can be just as disruptive as union activities in the plant. However, the right of the employee–union representative to engage in union activity during working hours but off the employer premises is almost invariably determined by some contract coverage or a practice acceptable to the parties. Such a dispute was resolved by a finding allowing union representatives to engage in such off-limits activity. The labor agreement granted employees the right within certain limits to be excused from work to attend to union business. In this instance, the employer denied union representatives requests to leave work to help in the union's organization efforts at a newly acquired sister company. The arbiter held, and rightly so, that the company had no right to deny the union's leave-of-absence request because it disapproved of the activity involved. The arbiter also considered management's denial unreasonable on its premise that the activity concerned union business outside the scope of the bargaining unit. A contract expression, "employees shall be granted leave of absence," could not be interpreted as confining union representatives to local activities which had a bearing solely upon the contractual relationship between these two parties.[15]

As mentioned before, interruptions of management's operations by union representatives takes numerous and various forms. A union official's aspirations for higher office may cause him to engage in activity which interferes with normal business functions. A job steward whose ambitions led him to seek a position as treasurer of his local union engaged in passing out election cards to fellow employees at the beginning of his work shift. Unquestionably union representatives do enjoy some immunity in carrying out their duties, particularly when involved in activities within the grievance procedure, and the individual here was a union representative. Further, he was not acting in an official capacity when he was passing out campaign materials proclaiming his qualifications for higher union office. Relevant contract clauses stated:

> Neither the union nor its members shall carry on union activities, including any election activities, on company premises or on company time.
> The company reserves the right to curtail or prohibit any union activity on any company premises when in its judgment such activity interferes with the normal use of the premises for their intended purposes.

It was plain that no union activities could be conducted on company premises or on company time, aside from certain solicitation of members and some forms of grievance handling. As the arbitrator rightly reflected, "This is almost as clear as contract language ever becomes."

Among the union's arguments was the claim that the contractual expression "election activities" referred only to actual elections. On this point, the arbiter said, "To say that the distribution of campaign material is not an election activity seems rather strained, but the point is not material. 'Election activities' are listed merely as one example of 'Union activities.' It is *union activities* per se which are prohibited, with the two noted exceptions, and not just election activities. Can the union contend that the distribution of union election cards was not a union activity? If he was not engaged in election activity, nor in any other type of union activity, it is difficult to know how else we might characterize his actions."[16]

When considering the problem of union activity during working hours, it is cases similar to the above about which management is most concerned. This type of electioneering activity is obviously involved solely with the internal functions of the labor organization. It is unique and peculiar to this organization and has no relatedness to the union-management relationship between the parties. It has nothing to do with the operation of the grievance machinery or the usual union representational activities which customarily occur under the labor agreement. It is plain that management is getting no return on its wage-dollar investment when an employee on his paid working time interrupts or interferes with other employees on paid working time. It is an irresponsible union which provokes labor-relations representatives to guard zealously against the threat of further union encroachments into paid union activities.

In a case decided by Arbitrator Joseph Shister, an employee was found to have violated a plant rule of an aircraft company by disobeying a superintendent's order to leave the place where a damaged helicopter was being unloaded from an airplane. The employee, although functioning in his other capacity as a union official, was nevertheless interrupting the unloading operation during an emergency situation. In this instance, the superintendent refused to discuss the grievance while the operation was going on, even though the complaint allegedly dealt with his working men out of classification on the unloading work. In discussing the "work interruption" aspect of this particular dispute, Arbitrator Shister made this comment:

Under normal circumstances the refusal of a supervisory employee to discuss with the appropriate Union official an actual or potential grievance can, in a specified setting, be construed as a refusal to bargain in good faith and would make it difficult for the union to "police the contract." But the circumstances under which G refused to discuss the problem in hand with L were anything but normal. A storm was on its way and valuable property had to be removed from the field before the storm actually broke. Time, in other words, was of the essence, which made it an emergency situation. Of course even in an emegency situation there might be a basis for an instance by a union official on discussing an actual or potential grievance if the failure so to discuss it would cause irreparable damage to the interest of the union or any of its members. But certainly this was not the situation in the instant case.[17]

A similar ruling was rendered by Arbitrator Michael I. Komaroff in a grievance between North American Aviation and the UAW. A union representative, a cashier in the plant cafeteria, demanded immediate relief from her job during a noon rush period to process a grievance, thereby holding up a line of employees for several minutes. The union's contention that the employee's demand was proper under a contract clause which provided that union representatives would be permitted to leave their jobs upon request was rejected by the arbitrator. His reasoning was comparable to that of Arbitrator Shister in the prior case:

> In the instant grievance it is necessary to ask the question: Would the effectiveness of investigation and settlement of the grievance concerning [a salaried employee's] working behind the cigar counter have been prejudiced in any way if [steward] had waited until she had checked out the line of employees before processing the grievance? No evidence whatever is submitted by the Union to establish that its interests and needs, or the processing of the grievance would have been detrimentally affected in any way. It is apparent, therefore, that a reasonable interpretation of Article V, Section 10 did not require supervision to instantly relieve [the steward] under the circumstances that existed at that time.
>
> On the basis of the above reasoning the Impartial Arbitrator concluded that the facts in this case do not establish a violation of Article V, Section 10 by the Company. On the contrary, [the steward] in completely ignoring the needs of efficient operation of the cafeteria, and incidentally the needs of the long line of employees waiting to be checked out, did interfere with plant efficiency.[18]

Another example of arbitral logic in this connection is illustrated in a case where a contract provision stated: "Either or both parties may with discretion call in witnesses to a grievance meeting." In this case, during a third-step grievance discussion the union president requested that the foreman of a discharged employee be called to the meeting. The company officials present at the meeting refused, stating that the foreman was attending a production meeting. When deciding the matter, the arbitrator made this comment:

> Since the main purpose of a factory is to produce goods, it would be proper to consider this clause in the light of that situation. Certainly, it would not be using discretion if the calling of witnesses would impede production or delay the process of manufacturing, since the hearing of grievances is not the primary purpose of such an organization. Further, to call witnesses "with discretion" would mean that they should not be called so that the conduct of the plant would be impaired by the absence of the witness from his proper work.
>
> It is, therefore, the opinion that both parties have the right to call witnesses, either supervisory or union employees to any grievance hearing, but that, if the calling of a particular witness would impede or slow down the production, then a refusal to call such witness at the time is not required, and the matter should be continued or delayed until such time as the witness is available for questioning. In the given instance, if the foreman was attending a production meeting then the refusal to call him would not be a violation of the Agreement, but at the same time there should have been an indication of when he would be available and the matter continued to such time.[19]

The solution in another case turned largely upon the significance of the word "reasonable" in a leave-of-absence provision of the contract. The language provided:

> *Leave for Union Activity*
>
> Leave of absence shall be extended to designated members of the union for union activities, and seniority shall accumulate during such leaves. Any employee who is a member of said union, and who may be called upon to transact business for said union or participate in any hearings or meetings outside the plant, upon *reasonable* notice to the proper representative of the company, be permitted to leave his work for time sufficient to transact such business or attend such meetings as may be necessary. The number of members on any such leave at any one time shall not exceed 50 nor more than one third of the employees in any one section.

Under the prior agreement, the identical provision had appeared without the word "reasonable." The company contended that under that prior contract various members of the union had engaged in a practice of giving brief notice to their foreman of their desire to leave work on union business and immediately doing so. The company further insisted that this type of disruption of production accounted for the insertion of the word "reasonable" into the agreement during collective bargaining. The arbitrator's finding was twofold. First, he concluded that this contract clause did not apply to union officials leaving their jobs to transact union business in the plant. This conclusion was drawn from the leave clause, which was so worded as to refer clearly to relatively long absences from the plant. Secondly, an examination of the contract grievance procedure disclosed that it adequately covered the question of leaving jobs for the purposes of handling grievances.

However, the second question of what "constituted reasonable notice" was a little more difficult to answer. Within the framework of this contract and perhaps with applicability to any other, the arbiter deemed the term "reasonable" as denoting a standard and felt that it should be taken to mean "reasonable under all of the attending circumstances." His evaluation of this term, which is commonly utilized by parties at the bargaining table but causes frequent consternation in determining its meaning, provides some interesting insights and merits a review:

> It is quite evident that reasonable notice on a day when there is an entirely adequate supply of skilled men or a surplus of production might be a matter of a few minutes or two or three hours. "Reasonable notice" that an officer of the union desired to leave the production line or plant on union business might also be very brief if there does, in fact, exist some type of vital dispute requiring his immediate attendance elsewhere in the interest of the union. On the other hand, "reasonable notice" might be a matter of several hours where the services of the man desiring leave are indispensable and production requirements depend heavily on his continuing the work. In other words, the term "reasonable" is not one which either side or in fact both sides, except by express understanding, can limit to an exact number of hours. The undersigned arbitrator cannot believe that the union, by consenting to the introduction of the disputed word in the contract at the point in question, agreed that a rule defining it as a period of 48 hours should be made solely at the discretion of the company.
> Even if the agreement can be read as the company interpreted it, the period of 48 hours seems to be unduly long in view of the type of business involved and its organization.[20]

Despite this ruling, he upheld disciplinary suspension of the local union president who deliberately violated the company's new rule requiring employees to give 48 hours' notice of their desire to be absent from their jobs for union business. This decision was in keeping with the well-established concept that (1) the propriety of a rule should be resolved in the contract's grievance procedure and (2) a union president has a special responsibility to be careful to observe contractual procedures and not resort to self-help.

Sometimes the question is not whether the union representative is engaged in "legitimate" union activity during working hours but what is he to be paid while so engaged. An employee who held a leadman classification was elected chairman of the union committee. The contract stated that a committeeman shall receive his "regular hourly rate" for all time spent on union business. Significant here was the fact that the employee's rate was established when he became chairman of the union committee. While the company argued that the employee did not earn his special leadman's rate unless he was available to "lead," it was also significant to the arbiter that the employee had been paid the leadman's rate for time spent in union business while he was a regular committeeman, plus receiving the same for his holidays and vacations. Moreover, an examination of past practice revealed that the chairman of the union committee, as elected by employees from any of the various classifications, had been paid his "regular hourly rate" in the past.[21]

Under an agreement that "union representatives shall be permitted to leave their respective jobs and-or departments when necessary for purpose of investigating or handling grievances," a question arose whether the union could appoint a steward to represent employees in a department other than the one in which he worked. In other words, could he represent more than one department? The company declined to recognize the individual who had been appointed steward in any department but his home one. Again, as in the prior cited cases, the arbitrator derived controlling guidance from certain contract language. In the relevant portions of this decision, he found the following conditions to govern the dispute:

> In the current Labor Agreement, the Parties negotiated a new section in Article IX known as Section 5. Neither this or any other similar section was contained in the prior Labor Agreement. It provides that "Union representatives shall be permitted to leave their respective jobs *and-or departments* when necessary for the purpose of investigating or handling grievances [emphasis supplied].
>
> The clear meaning of the new section must be that a departmental steward is authorized, after permission from his supervisor, to go out of his department into another department to conduct grievance handling.
>
> It must be remembered that the Union has the right to conduct its internal affairs in its own manner and unrestricted by the Company. The Labor Agreement does not authorize the Company to designate who shall be acceptable as departmental representatives; neither does it restrict the operation or appointment of a departmental steward to the department in which he works.
>
> It must, therefore, be the conclusion, based upon the evidence and the

provision of the Labor Agreement, that the appointment of PV as Department Representative of department 90 was made by proper union officials and that she is entitled to serve in that capacity and is further entitled to be recognized by the Company as the duly appointed departmental representative of her constituents in department 90.[22]

Under the National Labor Relations Act (NLRA), union representatives do not need to be employees of the company with whom the contract is made by the union. But customarily employment for many of the union's representatives has become a prerequisite. If the union demands that its representatives be union members, under the NLRA the employer must comply. And such a demand is commonly made. Nevertheless, in some rare instances unions have consented to have nonunion members act as stewards. Under the act, the employer cannot dictate to the employees whom they shall have as their bargaining or union representatives, nor can it interfere in any election. Many contracts are silent on the manner of selecting the union's representatives. So that the employer knows who the union representatives are, most contracts usually state that the union must provide a list of the representatives it has chosen. Usually the contract further provides that the union will keep the company informed on any changes it makes. Of course, the company should be so advised before the union's representatives assume their duties.

Although the employer has no right under the act to dictate who union representatives shall be, it would appear that it is given some voice in determining how many union representatives shall be selected among its employees. The reason for this is that union activities should not be conducted on company premises in a way that would interfere with industrial efficiency and discipline. The expeditious adjustment of labor disputes would be seriously hampered if the membership of union committees was so large as to render personal negotiations impossible. It also would be a heavy burden on industry if the number of stewards was out of proportion to the number of employees represented, particularly where stewards are paid by the employer for time spent in handling grievances. For these reasons, it is commonly left to the process of collective bargaining to determine the number of the union's representatives.[23]

Typically, labor agreements allow some form of payment to union representatives for time spent processing labor grievances. Also, it is not uncommon to find union representatives who like *unworked but paid union time*. In the absence of effective contractual control, grievances and the time necessary to dispose of them will expand to the maximum time the contract and management will allow for their investigation and discussion. The larger the amount of time allowed, the greater the time that will probably be spent by union representatives in grievance pursuits. There is no question that sufficient time to handle grievance matters effectively and adequately should be allowed and taken, but every grievance investigation and discussion, if not resolved, must reach the point where the parties are merely repeating themselves and rehashing arguments and positions. When this point is reached, no benefit is derived from continuing to argue the matter. At some point, management's representatives can sum up the company's position on the matter, indicating to the union representatives and the grievant what the disposition will be, and bring the discussion to a close.

One of the union's primary functions is the investigation of grievances. However, in its zeal it may occasionally spend unnecessary time in the pursuit of imaginary complaints or simply in the determination of whether the company is contemplating an action which may result in a contract violation. Disputes between the parties on this subject are commonplace since the union is almost invariably seeking more time (paid by the company) and the company typically wishes to keep it under tight control, limiting and restricting it as much as contractually and economically possible.

A final example is that of the International Harvester Company and the UAW, where a group of 14 employees left their jobs and went en masse to the foreman to express dissatisfaction with certain changed working conditions and piece-work prices they alleged were improper. The actions of the aggrieved, euphemistically called the presentation of a mass grievance, was ruled wrong by the arbitrator.

> And it was so precisely because it was designed to circumvent the jointly agreed to and established procedure for grievance settlement through the employment of a coercive tactic the use of which, at least in the settlement of day-to-day disputes subject to the jurisdiction of the Permanent Arbitrator, the contracting parties certainly must have intended to forego. While it is arguable whether in other circumstances, the contract may be said to preclude the presentation of oral complaints by more than one employee at the same time, it is inconceivable that in making provision for an *orderly* grievance procedure the contracting parties meant to sanction the oral presentation of a variety of grievances by 14 employees at the same time to the same foreman.[24]

In summing up this matter, it may be advisable to review those factors which have guided and influenced arbitrators' judgments as they relate to the operation of the contractual grievance machinery: (1) The underlying purpose of the grievance procedure is to provide an orderly and peaceful process for the prompt and expeditious resolution of disputes between the parties. (2) To accomplish this purpose, it must be administered in a plant climate where such grievances are filed, discussed, investigated, and processed with a minimum of disruption or interruption of the factory's operations. (3) At the same time, it must be accomplished in a manner which does not produce, or result in, an impairment of the union's ability and right to represent its members.

Under most agreements, the union's representatives are required to work at their assigned jobs at all times except when they are needed to handle grievances. Only then are they privileged to leave their assignments to handle grievances. It is also not uncommon for such grievance handling to occur during the employees' working hours. When occasions arise which require grievance handling during working hours, as it is inevitable they will, some procedure should be understood which allows this without a disruptive influence on production operations. But despite an established procedure, both parties must be aware that no system can be completely foolproof. There may be times when difficulties arise which will be hard to classify under any system. The parties should be able reasonably to adjust their differences whenever and wherever they occur. However, we are dealing here in an area where abuses can occur. Stewards sometimes may look upon their office as a means to escape assigned productive work. One who uses more time than is reasonably necessary for the handling of a union matter embarrasses his union and abuses the privileges of his office.

The grievance machinery is the formal process, preliminary to any arbitration, which enables the parties to attempt to resolve their differences peacefully and in an orderly, expeditious manner. It permits the company and the union to investigate and discuss problems without interruption to the continued orderly operation of the business. And working effectively, with good faith practiced by both parties, it can bring about the satisfactory resolution of the overwhelming majority of disputes.

Chapter 3
Company Pay for Union Time

It is common to find union representatives who enjoy unworked time (spent in the pursuit of union activities) which is paid for by the company. In the absence of foreman control, grievances and the time spent by union representatives in connection with them will expand to fill the time management allows for their investigation and discussion. The greater the amount of time allowed by the company, the greater the time spent by union representatives in their pursuit.

The problem of payment to union representatives for time spent on grievances has been dealt with in various ways. However, there are no clearly established patterns. An examination of a number of labor agreements covering a variety of industries reveals that such matters are usually covered by contractual provisions which specify the extent of the company's liability, if any. Also, they often provide safeguards designed to protect against the extension of grievance payments to other situations not contemplated by the contract. Generally, labor agreements contain some provision which allows authorized and designated union representatives reasonable time, without any loss of pay, to facilitate the processing of grievances where a detailed grievance procedure is outlined in the contract. Frequently a clause may limit the pay for time spent by union representatives in handling grievances to "a reasonable number of hours each week." In many cases, it further authorizes the company to require the union representative to submit reports which account for the paid time expended on grievance problems.

Typical of a contract where paid union time is stipulated is the national labor agreement of the General Electric Company. Article 12, "Payment for Time on Local Union Activities," provides that the company will pay for absences from work for union officers while engaged in processing grievances on the company's premises. This agreement contains a schedule of payments when the activity falls within the defined steps of the grievance procedure. It also contains limitations. An example of this is that the payment to stewards is limited to two hours per week. The payment to union committee members also has limitations. All union representatives entitled to payments by the company for grievance time are required to file a report accounting for their time to their departmental foreman. It further requires that they must advise their foreman before leaving their job to engage in union activity. These are merely a few examples of the elements of this contract relevant to the discussion here. Additionally, the General Electric contract contains other provisions designed to control the time expended on grievances by union representatives paid for by the company.

Another issue often dealt with by arbitrators is the question of the difference, if any, between "time lost" and "time consumed in handling grievances." If the labor agreement or some controlling past practice allows the payment to union representatives for "time lost" in the pursuit of grievances, such contract language has not been construed to require payment by the company for time spent by union representatives after their regular working hours. This is so unless the contract or a controlling past practice clearly demonstrated an intent by both parties to the contrary. The terms "time lost" and "time consumed" have not been deemed synonymous by arbitrators. Therefore, in the absence of a clear intention to the contrary, the company's payment to union representatives for time spent on grievances has not been extended to time spent after the regular working hours. This has been the ruling by a great majority of arbitrators.

In 1980, the Bureau of National Affairs studied over 400 agreements then in effect with regard to trends in grievance procedures. Their findings are reported in "Basic Patterns in Labor Agreements" (34LA931). With regard to pay practices for grievance activity under these agreements, the report revealed the following:

> About 51 percent of contracts now provide pay to employees who function as union officials in presenting, investigating, and processing grievances—an increase of one quarter over 1977. About a fourth of the agreements providing pay for grievance activity are carefully worded to restrict compensation to time spent in conferences with management in connection with the adjustment of grievances. At least some of the time required for the investigation of grievances is paid for under half of such contracts. The rest are somewhat vague in this respect, stating only that union representatives will be paid for time spent in "handling and processing" grievances. Just under one of every four contracts providing pay for grievance representatives places a ceiling on management's liability for grievance pay. This may be done in any of three ways—(1) by limiting the number of individuals who may collect grievance pay, (2) by limiting the time that may be spent on grievance matters, or (3) by limiting the pay for

time so spent. In addition, a few agreements impose a general limitation by reserving management's right to restrict the amount of time off with pay, either in whole or in part, in the event of unreasonable use of the privilege.

Only 6 percent of contracts specifically provide pay to employees involved in grievance-adjustment proceedings. Where grievance meetings are held during working hours, however, employees frequently are paid as a matter of plant practice, despite contractual silence on the point.

Six percent of contracts state that grievance representatives will not be paid for time spent in this part of their union job. At the other extreme, only one agreement in the sample provides for fulltime comapny-paid union grievance representatives.[1]

From reading this survey, it is clear that the amount of time, if any, which the company will compensate union representatives in their prosecution of grievances is a negotiable issue decided between the parties in the process of collective bargaining. The labor agreement is therefore the source of any such right enjoyed by the union and only to the extent that it so provides is the company obligated for such payments.

Generally, but with certain exceptions, where the contract is silent, past practice is held to govern whether the union representative–employee should be compensated for time lost from work for the grievance procedure. Most arbitrators have reasoned that by making *no* provision in the contract for either a payment or a denial of pay for such time, the parties have indicated that they were content to let the matter rest on the basis of whatever the existing practice was. But where the practice clearly indicates an abuse of the privilege, the company has been held justified for refusing to pay for such excess grievance time.

There is little question that unions generally favor the principle of company pay for grievance work. They often argue this on the ground that adjustment of grievances is also a service to the company and therefore the company should pay for it. On the other side of this issue, the company usually argues that it is engaged in a business relationship with the union which imposes a commensurate obligation on the union to operate and behave in a businesslike manner. Their contention further says that attendant to this business obligation of the union is a duty to stand on its own two feet and pay its own representatives for their grievance time.

On occasion an employer has argued that the terms of the Labor-Management Reporting and Disclosure Act, specifically Section 505, which amended Section 302 of the Labor Management Relations Act, makes it unlawful for an employer to compensate union officers for time spent in handling grievances.

Section 302 of the Labor Management Relations Act, as amended (Public Law 86-257, 29USC 185), provides in part:

Sec. 302. (a) It shall be unlawful for any employer or association of employers or any person who acts as a labor relations expert, adviser, or consultant to an employer or who acts in the interest of an employer to pay, lend, or deliver, or agree to pay, lend, or deliver, any money or other thing of value—

(1) to any representative or any of his employees who are employed in an industry affecting commerce; or

(2) to any labor organization, or any officer or employee thereof, which represents, seeks to represent, or would admit to membership, any of the employees of such employer who are employed in an industry affecting commerce; or

(3) to any employee or group or committee of employees of such employer employed in an industry affecting commerce in excess of their normal compensation for the purpose of causing such employee or group or committee directly or indirectly to influence any other employees in the exercise of the right to organize and bargain collectively through representatives of their own choosing; or

(4) to any officer or employee of a labor organization engaged in an industry affecting commerce with intent to influence him in respect to any of his actions, decisions, or duties as a representative of employees or as such officer or employee of such labor organization....

(b) (1) It shall be unlawful for any person to request, demand, receive, or accept, or agree to receive or accept, any payment, loan, or delivery of any money or other thing of value prohibited by subsection (a)....

(c) The provisions of this section shall not be applicable (1) in respect to any money or other thing of value payable by an employer to any of his employees whose established duties include acting openly for such employer in matters of labor relations or personnel administration or to any representative of his employees, or to any officer or employee of a labor organization, who is also an employee or former employee of such employer, as compensation for, or by reason of, his service as an employee of such employer....

(d) Any person who willfully violates any of the provisions of this section shall, upon conviction thereof, be guilty of a misdemeanor and be subject to a fine of not more than $10,000 or to imprisonment for not more than one year, or both.

This question has been the central issue in some arbitration cases and has been reviewed by various competent and reputable arbitrators.[2] It should be understood that an arbitration award interpreting the law would not preclude a court from making a contrary interpretation and that a decision of such a court on a question of legality would take precedence over an arbiter's award. An arbitration award may be erroneous for many reasons, mistakes of fact or law, and still enforceable because the parties have agreed that it shall be final and binding, but no award can impart legality to an illegal act and preclude a court of competent jurisdiction from declaring the act illegal.[3]

But in those arbitration cases where opinions on this point have been expressed, there is a unanimity of viewpoint: The law was not designed to prohibit payment to union stewards for time spent in processing grievances where such payment is required by the contract or past practice. The purpose of the law is to prohibit payments by an employer to labor organizations or their officers in excess of their normal compensation where such payment is designed to influence the employee's fair representation or right to organize and bargain collectively. The clear intent of the law is to make it a criminal offense for an employer to attempt to bribe a union officer or to induce him to corrupt and subvert the legitimate right of employees to organize and bargain collectively.

Lost time cannot be considered in excess of normal compensation. Although a union officer attending to a grievance is not engaged in normal productive work, he is nevertheless rendering service which is regarded as within the course and scope of his employment.

Where payment for such time is required under the terms of the agreement or is established by custom or practice, it is not in conflict with any of the provisions of the Labor-Management Reporting and Disclosure Act. The act contemplates, and was never intended to prohibit, the widespread practice of paying employees–union representatives where such payments have been agreed upon in collective bargaining. This includes not only the actual time spent in conferring with management but any scheduled time such employee loses incidental to his grievance-adjustment activity.

In this connection, the union has often argued (I believe persuasively) that such payments agreed upon during collective bargaining are no more illegal than company payments for coffee breaks, lunch periods, sick leaves, holidays, vacations, jury duty. No court that I know of has found any of these violative of the Labor Management Relations Act except when they are accompanied by other acts of company domination or some other form of illegal support of the union.

It can be stated with some degree of certainty that this is so because of a contrary provision in Section 8(a)(2) of the same act: "An employer shall not be prohibited from permitting employees to confer with him during working hours without loss of time or pay."

To support further the conclusion that the act condones and permits such payments, an examination of the legislative history of the act may prove productive. It is safe to say that the congressional inquiry in 1959, and the resulting amendments to this act, were primarily concerned with gifts, bribes, blackmail, and particularly payments to trust funds. Prior to that time, and since, company payments to employee–union representatives were, and are, widespread. It is apparent that Congress did not intend to make them illegal. The only logical conclusion that can be reached is that the legislators were aware of such company payments, saw nothing wrong with them, did not specifically condemn them, and did not believe it necessary to change the law since the law already permitted them.[4]

Final evidence in support of this conclusion came from the Bureau of Labor Statistics (BLS) in Bulletin 1266, "Company Pay for Time Spent on Union Business." This comprehensive and authoritative report was issued in 1959, just one month after passage of the Section 302 amendments. This survey analyzed 1,631 major labor agreements, each of which covered 1,000 or more employees, a total of 7.5 million workers, nearly 50 percent of the number of workers covered by all labor agreements. Of these 1,631 contracts, BLS reported that about 40 percent of the contracts, covering over 3 million workers, contained some provision for the full or partial payment to union representatives for time spent by them on grievance activity.

Another interesting aspect of Bulletin 1266 is its comments (p. 2) regarding the significance of past practice under the contract:

> It is important to note that this study relates only to pay provisions established under terms of collective bargaining agreements and does not take into account informal arrangements where the employee or union representative is permitted to have his work for union business without a reduction in pay. The practice of granting time off without loss of pay while engaged in union activities – at least those activities which are of concern to both company and union – is undoubtedly more widespread than a study of formal contract provisions would indicate. In many instances, it is likely that a contract provision was negotiated to define or limit an existing informal practice, rather than to establish a new practice.

Disputes between the parties on the matter of company payments for union time are commonplace since the union almost invariably seeks more time paid by the company, the company typically trying to keep it under tight control. At the least, the employer is always desirous to limit and restrict it. Typical of this type of dispute was one between Bendix Aviation Corporation and the International Union of Electrical Workers. Discussing the particular fact situation, the arbitrator made this observation:

> Under this and other sections of the collective bargaining agreement, the union claims that inherent therein is the right to police the collective bargaining agreement and to properly police it, the union must have free and unrestricted access to all parts of the plant.
>
> As I read the agreement, investigative rights by stewards, and so forth, is limited to those situations where a grievance or dispute *already* exists. There is nothing in the collective bargaining agreement which gives these union representatives the right to roam about the plant seeking a possible violation of the agreement.
>
> To permit this might well create an intolerable condition. The right to police the contract which is inherent in most agreements does not extend that far. Its limit, as here, is to police *only* when a grievance or dispute has arisen.[5]

It appears that the union was seeking a right to go on fishing expeditions, and as mentioned earlier, thereby have their problems expand to fill more fully whatever company-paid time would be allowed.

A good example of the impact past practice can have on a dispute in this area is illustrated in a case involving Industrial Rayon and the Textile Workers Union. The labor agreement contained a comprehensive grievance procedure that was silent with regard to payment for time spent by union officials in the processing of grievances. No prior agreement had contained express provision for such payments. The evidence established that for several years preceding the dispute the company had paid for grievance time, notwithstanding the absence of express contract language. This practice had evidently been in existence for about 15 years, and apparently the subject matter had not been discussed or included in the agenda of the succeeding contract negotiations.

The grievance stemmed from an announced policy on the part of the company restricting and limiting the amount of compensation for which the company would be obligated for time spent in processing grievances. The effect of the announced policy was to curtail substantially the extent of the company's financial obligation for grievance time. Basically, the issue was whether the company was required to continue all of the past practices in paying for grievance time. The union contended the past practice was well established and constituted a condition of employment which might not be unilaterally terminated. In reviewing this matter, the arbitrator made the following observation:

> The claims of the Company that there was no contractual obligation to continue the practice, and that its payment in the past had been voluntary and "tolerated" do not serve to negate the fact that such payment had been adhered to for so long a period, as to ripen into a condition of employment which may not be unilaterally abolished. Any substantive changes or

departure from the established pattern would necessarily have to be the subject of collective bargaining and negotiation during the life of the labor agreement. Since there was no effort to eliminate the practice during successive contract negotiations there developed a tacit consent to continue the practice. Under these circumstances, the Company would be deemed estopped from discontinuing this "condition of employment" during the life of the contract.[6]

This type of situation is caused by acquiescence to behavior by employees, or as in this case, to the conduct, behavior, and demands of union representatives. The union should not be blamed in a case such as this. It can hardly be blamed for accepting payment for union time from the company rather than going unpaid or having to reimburse itself via the union treasury. The behavior is simply true to human nature and is wholly in accord with motivations and objectives as union representatives. The fault rests solely within the company's power to grant or withhold it. But obviously, once having granted it and repeated it through the term of several agreements, the company finally was as locked in to make such payments as if there were explicit language requiring it. There lies the danger. Neither should the arbitrator be faulted. He is merely rendering a decision in accord with the overwhelming arbitral authority. The union is not to blame, nor is the arbitrator at fault. *The single party responsible for this predicament is the party which gave life and continuity to the practice – the company.*

The amount of time for which the company will compensate union representatives in their prosecution of grievances is a negotiable issue decided between the parties in practice or in bargaining. The labor agreement is therefore the source of any such rights enjoyed by the union, and only to the extent that it so provides is the company obligated for such payments.

One last point in this connection: Where under the contract or past practice union officers are granted pay for "time lost" in handling grievances, the language is not construed to require pay for time spent *after* regular working hours. Arbitrators have held that "time lost" is not synonymous with "time consumed" and that unless the contract or past practice evidences a clear intent to the contrary, the payment for time spent in handling grievances may not be extended to time spent after regular working hours.[7]

Occasionally the parties arbitrate a dispute over the company's requirement to pay union officials for time spent in contract negotiations. Under an agreement between the United Carbon Company and the Oil Workers, the union insisted that past practice entitled them to this company payment. The company protested the past practice on two counts: (1) The contract language was clear and unambiguous. (2) Payments in the past had been purely voluntary manifestations of goodwill. After examining the entire agreement, the arbitrator could find no violations and denied the grievance.[8]

Another question which sometimes arises between the parties is whether the agreement contemplates company payment to union representatives for time spent in arbitration hearings. Under a contract where the grievance-procedure clause provided that "time spent during regular working hours by stewards or chief stewards in investigating and disposing of grievances will be paid for by the Company," the union contended this language provided coverage of arbitration hearings. In denying the union's grievance and ruling that the clause did not entitle union representatives to this payment, the arbitrator considered it significant that the arbitration clause made no mention of pay for time spent at such hearings. And since the arbitration and grievance procedures were set out in different sections of the contract, they had to be considered as separate provisions for purposes of contract interpretation.[9]

It has also been held that the company would not have the right unilaterally to promulgate a rule which specified the maximum time union representatives would be compensated for in the handling of grievances where the contract provided pay for time spent in grievance processing without mentioning any limitation. In this situation, the past practice for a considerable period of time had been to pay for all time spent in grievance activity. However, the arbitrator said that the company had the right to challenge union representatives in specific instances where it questioned the reasonableness of the time they were claiming for grievance activity.[10]

These cases materially differ from one where an employer informed the union prior to its election of officers that it was going to cease paying union officers for time spent in committee meetings. The committee meetings were used to supervise the company's contemplation of layoff and recall procedures and processing and handling grievances. This rule was initiated by the employer in mid-contract term. The arbitrator ruled that the union representatives were entitled to pay for time thus spent, up to the expiration date of the current contract. The payment was disallowed after the effective date of a subsequent contract which contained no provision for such payment. The arbitral theory concluded that the prior practice of granting such payment could be terminated by the employer, but only after notice to the union and the termination of the existing contract. The union's failure to negotiate a provision continuing the practice resulted in a termination of the company's obligation.[11]

It must be realized that when we are dealing with the procedure for settling grievances, the conditions of this process must not be so onerous as to impair its flexibility and effectiveness. But when the contract contains an obligation for the company to pay for certain union time, the company has a right to expect a full and accurate account of that time. Such a relation of duty and right carries with it, in the absence of a fairly clear contractual exclusion, a right to demand that only contractually sanctioned time be spent during working hours on union business paid by the company. What accounting should be demanded? The answer in a general sense is a reasonable accounting. The nature of each grievance should usually reveal who must be involved, where the investigation must occur, and about how much time will be necessary to give it adequate coverage. If the time spent on a grievance by a union representative appears to be excessive, the foreman should require him to substantiate his alleged use of time, and if he fails to provide a reasonably credible accounting, the foreman may refuse to authorize payments or may elect to institute some disciplinary measure, particularly in the face of continuous and flagrant abuses.

Of course, these are not the only type of problem encountered by supervision in their attempts to control union time. Another example of what may happen is illustrated in a case involving General Electric and the UAW where the company suspended a union-shop committee chairman for one week for continuing to mark on his production work slip time that had actually been spent on union business and should have been indicated on a separate slip. In this instance the contract contained a specific provision relating to time spent during working hours by union officers on union business and limited the time that would be paid. Secondly, claiming such time as productive time gave a false picture of the union officer's actual productivity and could cause inaccurate production records. The arbitrator, Daniel P. Kornblum, made the following comments:

> The Arbitrator has no doubt that the grievant was a most zealous and dedicated union functionary in the shop. Nor has he doubt as to the grievant's complete honesty in trying to fulfill his demanding dual role as both Shop Chairman and working employee. But as has been observed in a number of arbitration decisions factually akin to this, an employee's status as a union official does not "immunize" him from disciplinary action as an employee for infractions like these presented in this record.
>
> It remains too, that the Agreement makes explicit provision as to the conditions and limitations of the Company's obligation to pay for time lost in handling grievances. In light then of the provision in the Agreement which denies the Arbitrator "authority to add to, detract from, or in any

way alter the provisions of this Agreement," the Arbitrator is powerless
to broaden the Company's obligation to pay for lost time on grievances.
*More importantly, the need accurately to distinguish between work time
and grievance handling time is implicit in the very nature of the limitations,* obviously if there is a ceiling on the Company's obligation to pay for
such lost time the Company has a right to insist that the distinction between work time and grievance time be properly reflected on its time
tickets.[12]

This type of dispute is commonplace. The union may claim that any
accounting or reporting system which requires that names and details be
supplied to the company offends the principle of the grievance procedure
by exposing names of employees whose grievances may never reach
management. The union will argue that it does a service in eliminating
"fancied" grievances of employees without going to management. And
this may be true. But if there are large numbers of these "fancied"
grievances which involve a lot of time, it is obvious that the company is
entitled to know about them in order to eliminate the source of the fanci-
fulness.

With regard to any payments made to union representatives, Section 8(a)(2) of the act provides that an employer may pay employees for
time spent meeting on company property to process girevances with
members of management or in labor negotiations.[13] However, the company should refrain from paying employees for time spent in discussing
or engaging in internal union affairs.[14]

In some cases, where the employee–union representative fails to respond to a reasonable appeal from the company to limit his paid time on
union business to legitimate and contractually approved activity, the
employer may introduce a system of time recording and instruct the
employee to utilize it. Failing or refusing to do so, the union representative subjects himself to corrective forms of disciplinary action. Such a
time-reporting system requires the employee to record, on forms furnished by the company, information similar to the following: clock time
onto union business, department visited, time entered, time left, supervisor's signature of approval in department visited, names of persons
conversed with, nature and number of grievances discussed, clock time
returned to home department. Such a form is typically made out daily
and submitted to the company. In conjunction with this form, the
employee–union representative must first obtain permission from his
supervisor to leave his workplace, advising him of his destination and the
nature of the union activity. His supervisor telephones the department
to be visited and obtains clearance for the steward to visit that area. The

supervisor in the receiving department can then note the time of the steward's arrival and regulate his time and activity after arrival. When the steward is leaving that area, that supervisor can repeat the advance-telephoning process to the next area to be visited or call the home department, advising the home supervisor that the steward is returning to work.

It also is not uncommon to find labor agreements which deny payments of any kind to union representatives while they are involved in grievance prosecution. Representative of this is the type of provision which reads:

> If any Steward of the Union shall so request of his foreman, he shall be granted such time off *without pay* as may be reasonably required for the purpose of investigating the facts with regard to any Grievance in Step 1 or Step 2 presented by any employee in his department.
>
> If any member of the Grievance Committee shall so request of his foreman, he shall be granted time off *without pay* as may be reasonably required for the purpose of investigating the facts with regard to any Grievance in Step 3 or Step 4 with which he is concerned.

Such an agreement would also typically contain another catchall clause which would be intended to embrace all forms of union activity. It would probably read: "No employee shall engage in any union activity on the property of the Company in any manner which shall interfere with production, nor engage in any union activity on Company paid time."

Now let's examine four other cases with slightly different twists which set each apart from prior ones reviewed. Under the first, the contract stated: "The company will allow pay to working employees who are union representatives for loss of work time when attending scheduled grievance meetings with company representatives during their regularly scheduled working hours." The parties customarily held weekly grievance meetings where the order of grievances discussed was controlled by the union.

All but the last grievance had been discussed, and when it came time for it, the union raised the question whether union officers who would be required to be called to the meeting would be paid overtime. The company's answer was negative. In consequence, the union postponed the hearing of that grievance to a later date. At this point, the company advised the union that it did not intend to pay the union representatives for time they had spent awaiting their turn to meet and discuss this last grievance. Although the contract was clear in its allowance of pay to union representatives for time spent attending scheduled grievance meetings, the arbitrator ruled against the union's claim.

Attention is invited to the fact that there is nothing in this [contract] section that specifically requires the company to pay union section officers for time spent by them at a grievance meeting *waiting* for the grievance that they are processing to be heard. However, as a matter of practice, the company has paid for waiting time, *when and only when* the specific grievance that said union section officers are processing has been heard. Under these circumstances, there seems to be no contractual obligation, nor past practice on the part of the company for compensating union section officers when the grievance that they are processing has not been heard because the union has postponed the hearing of said grievance.[15]

In a second case, the contract granted pay to union stewards who attended grievance meetings "requested by the company during working hours." A steward was told not to report for his regular shift the next day but to report to the company's industrial-relations office where he was given a disciplinary suspension for leaving his job early contrary to his foreman's orders. The union claimed pay for him for his attendance at this disciplinary meeting; the company refused.

Arbitrator Whitley McCoy decided that the grievant was not entitled to payment for attendance at this meeting since he was not called to this meeting as a union steward but as an employee about to be disciplined. This was so although the steward had not been told in advance. The arbiter reasoned that there was no reasonable cause for the steward to mistake the purpose of the meeting since he had prior knowledge of the fact that he had been caught disobeying the foreman's orders.[16]

In another dispute, employees refused to work overtime while contract negotiations were going on. The company secured a temporary restraining order against this concerted refusal. The court issued an order that employees should appear in court to show cause why they should not be issued a temporary injunction banning the refusal. Some 120 employees of the company were requested to appear in court and asked that the company pay them for the time lost from work as a result of their being required to appear in court. The contract language here stated: "An employee who during his scheduled working hours meets with the company officials on grievances or other pertinent union business shall be paid at this regular hourly rate for time so spent."

The union contended under the "pertinent union business" portion of this language that the 120 employees should be paid for the time they lost. In finding for the company, the arbitrator concluded:

With respect to article 22 (e), it is the view of the referee that the situation which we have here before us is not covered by this article. Paragraph (e), it appears to the referee, relates to the normal processing of union grievances and the handling of other similar union business. It would be stretching paragraph (e) excessively, in the opinion of the referee, to construe it to mean that the company is required to pay for time lost by employees when, because of employee misconduct, workers are called into court.[17]

Arbitrators' decisions are influenced by past practice and the parties' history of negotiations. Under a contract, union officials were entitled to payment for time spent away from their jobs performing "functions" under the grievance procedure. The chairman of the Grievance Committee would be responsible for "submitting" to management grievances appealed from Step 2 to Step 3 of the grievance procedure by the union. It was ruled the grievance committee chairman was *not* entitled to pay for time spent in "writing" third-step appeals. The arbiter viewed the contract as ambiguous, but examination of the history of negotiations indicated the word *submitting* was intended to mean the act of delivering the third-step appeals to management. Influencing his opinion was the fact that the union made no claim for such payment for time spent "writing" third-step appeals until more than three years after the language had been adopted.[18]

In order for union representatives to receive compensation for time spent on union business, it may be necessary for them first to supply certain information to the employer. This happened under an agreement between Marlin-Rockwell Co. and the UAW. This contract contained provisions which provided the company with the right to require additional information relative to union officers processing grievances. The additional information referred to here was the name of the grievant and the nature of his grievance. The additional information was not considered by the arbitrator as any different from production or other records the company had a right to order to compensate employees properly for actual work performed. Second, requiring the submission of such additional information could not be considered as obstructing or interfering with the union officials' right to pursue their activities because such requirement constituted a reasonable administrative measure, particularly where the time spent in handling grievances is paid for by the employer. Neither did this requirement infringe upon any employee's right to a grievance since any with a legitimate grievance should not have objection to disclosure of his name or the nature of his grievance. Guided by the language of this contract, the arbitrator considered it immaterial that the company would be able to obtain this additional information from written grievances which had been filed during the second step of the grievance procedure.[19]

The question of whether an employee violated a contract provision prohibiting discrimination against employees because of union activities resulted when the company refused to pay 12 of 15 employees for time spent at a "special" union meeting on the company's premises. The company's payment to only three of these employees was made because they were the only ones who punched the time clock at the beginning of their shift. The other 12 employees had failed to clock in at the beginning of the shift, and thus it was impossible for the company to determine whether they were available for work from the actual starting time of their shift. The arbiter upheld the company's position.[20]

A company's negligence in asserting its right to certain controls over paid union time under an agreement produced a costly practice which the arbitrator held could not be unilaterally overturned. This labor agreement required the union "preceptor" to spend each morning walking through the plant to see if any grievances had arisen. This had been a daily practice of his, without first obtaining specific permission to do so, and he had been paid by the company for these visitations for a five-year period. Therefore, although he had not obtained expressed permission as required by the contract, the employer's knowledge of this fact was taken as tacit approval, which gave rise to a past practice that could not be stopped unilaterally by the company.[21]

Although sometimes management will pay union representatives for participation in arbitration hearings, it is not common. In the overwhelming majority of instances, once the parties have exhausted the regular grievance procedure and the case has been appealed to arbitration, any expenses relative to preparation and presentation in the actual arbitration hearing are costs each party assumes. Such payment was the issue under an agreement stating "each committee member and steward shall be allowed all necessary company time in adjusting grievances and time spent with company officials." While time spent in an arbitration hearing ordinarily would not be considered as time spent in "adjusting grievances" or "meeting with company officials," the contract language was construed by an arbitrator as not clearly and unequivocally excluding its application to a situation such as attendance at an arbitration hearing. In view of what he considered to be an ambiguity, he resolved the dispute by requiring the company to pay for working time lost by union officials attending arbitration hearings on the premise that the past practice under this provision in prior contracts between the parties had been to pay for such time. This practice was controlling.[22]

Under another agreement that provided that each party would pay its own expenses, the employer was held warranted in denying compensation to union officials for working time spent attending to matters required by the arbitration procedure. While the parties equally shared the charges and expenses of the arbitrator, the union failed to establish any conclusive past practice which called for lost-time compensation. In addition to being negated by a contract provision the union's claim was also inconsistent with widespread usual practices in American industry.[23]

While arbitration is in one sense a part of the grievance procedure, it is also a different kind of procedure than that involved in the earlier steps of the grievance procedure. There is no reason why a grievance procedure cannot exist without a provision for arbitration, and there are a few agreements that are thus constructed. In grievance meetings an effort is made to determine the facts and to arrive at some settlement or disposition of the grievance by agreement between representatives of the company and those of the union. But if such meetings are productive and result in disposition or settlement of the grievance, it is the product of such discussion and agreement, and not the consequence of adjudication. On the other hand, the arbitration procedure is a step beyond the grievance procedure. In that forum an impartial third party hears the arguments and the evidence of the management and the union and renders a decision which becomes binding on both parties.

Chapter 4
Union Access to Plant

Eminent authorities in the field of industrial relations have written that a union acquires certain rights upon the execution of a labor agreement. The right to bargain collectively for employees included in the bargaining unit is expressly provided in Sections 8(a) and 8(b)(3) of the National Labor Relations Act, as amended. Another function accorded a certified union is the right to police a collective bargaining agreement. This right flows from the recognition clause and from the inclusion of a grievance procedure in the contract. It can accomplish this only by being permitted to enter upon the company premises where such alleged grievances are taking place for making its investigation.

Often the question turns on the right of a union representative to reenter the plant on a shift other than the one on which he works. However, the right to go into the company's plant, irrespective of the wishes of the company, must be found by expressed or implied authority in the labor agreement or authority of law. On the question of whether Sections 7 and 8 of the National Labor Relations Act grant such a right, irrespective of the wishes of the company, the answer must be no.

A careful study of the arbitration cases on this question reveals that in every dispute where the union official was admitted to the company's property over the company's protest, the labor agreement expressly gave the union official the right to do so. No cases held to the contrary.

Sections 7 and 8 of the National Labor Relations Act are annotated in 29 Federal Code Annotated and 29 United States Code Annotated, Sections 157 and 158. Of the many hundreds of decisions by the National Labor Relations Board and by state and federal courts referred to under these sections, not one was found which sustains the proposition that the union official may have access to the company's property as a result of this law. To provide an overview of how arbitrators have interpreted "access to plant" provisions of an agreement, a few case histories are worthy of review.

In a case between Alcoa and the UAW, Arbitrator Paul Prasow was called upon to decide whether the company had raised a legitimate barrier to a union representative's access to the plant when it denied access on the basis that a bona fide grievance was not involved, as alleged, but was merely a pretext to gain entry for an entirely different matter. The contract language in this case was worded as follows:

Section 3. Access to Plants

An International Representative of the Union shall be granted access to plants of the company for the purpose of investigating grievances which are being considered by the Union and the Company at the final step of the Grievance Procedure, provided such investigations do not conflict with any governmental regulations and are in accordance with general rules agreed upon by the company and the union.[1]

Arbitrator Prasow made these observations:

The Arbitrator is in full agreement with the Company that plant entry on the part of Union representatives to investigate grievances should be limited to bona fide grievances. The union's right of access is predicated on the assumption that the Union should have an equal opportunity with management to investigate the circumstances surrounding a specific grievance at first hand, to interview the employees involved, and to examine other factors generally which are related to the issues involved in the grievance. This legitimate function is recognized in the Agreement by Sec. 3, and enables the Union to gather the information necessary to a proper handling or disposition of grievance matters.

The right of entry, however, does not imply that the Union's international representative may wander about at will, or perform functions other than those directly related to the investigation of a specific grievance which has been processed to the final step of the Grievance Procedure. Whether or not the Company questions the motives of the Union in regard to the investigation of a given grievance, the Company is within its rights in restricting or limiting the movements and activities of the Union's International Representative to investigation of the specific grievance under consideration.

On the other hand, there is nothing in the language of Sec. 3 which authorized the Company to deny plant access to a designated International Representative of the Union who requests entry to investigate a duly filed and processed grievance, which has reached the final step of the Grievance Procedure. To deny the union representative plant access under such circumstances would in effect empower the Company to unilaterally set itself up as the sole judge of which grievances are proper and which are not. Such unilateral determination could conceivably halt the processing of any grievance on the grounds that it was not filed in good faith. The principle at issue here is of the utmost importance, for the heart of a collective bargaining agreement after it has once been negotiated, and its continuing life, lies in the grievance procedure. To permit either party to unilaterally determine whether a grievance is bona fide, prior to exhausting all the steps of the grievance procedure, could seriously weaken or destroy the whole purpose and intent of the grievance procedure.

Seldom is a case brought to arbitration by the company filing a grievance against the union. On one such infrequent occasion, a company filed a grievance which stated in substance that the union's business agent had abused the contract's visitation privilege when he made excessive visits of excessive duration. This occurred where the labor agreement between the parties contained a section which reads:

> The union representatives shall be permitted to enter the building during working hours, entering the front office and signing in and out in order to interview the shop stewards or members working on the job. The union representatives shall not interfere with the progress of the work, but shall call the attention of the superintendent or foreman to any violation of this agreement.

Motivated by belief this contract privilege was being abused in an attempt to establish controls covering visits of the business agent to the plant, the company set up a series of rules:

1. Company to be notified of purposed visits and persons to be seen.
2. Passes to be prepared at front office for union representatives.
3. Union representatives to be allowed a reasonable amount of time for visits.
4. Company to have the right to send an escort with the business agent or to have the person to be interviewed brought to the office.

The union protested these rules violated its rights under the section above. The company claimed that many or most of the visits of the business agent did not result in the filing of grievances. They further contended his visits interfered with production. The company also contended it had a perfect right to require nonemployees to state fully whom they intended to see and where they intended to go.

The union claimed that during negotiation of the agreement the company attempted to insert a requirement that the business agent state the department and person he intended to see. It further claimed that the union refused to agree to this proposal and the provisions of the section were agreed to instead of the company's proposal. They said that now the company was attempting to alter the terms of the agreement. In finding for the Union, the arbitrator considered the following the controlling factors:

> The chairman has carefully reviewed the evidence in this case. While the company has charged that Mr. ____'s visits have interfered with production, no specific proof of this was presented at the hearing. Likewise, the company agreed at the hearing that on many occasions Mr. ____ was called to the plant by them. . . .
>
> Now when we examine the language of Section 10, it mentions only a requirement that union representatives sign in and sign out, nothing is said about stating to whom they intend to go or any other requirements, except that the progress of the work is not to be interfered with. *The parties by specifying a procedure to be followed must have intended to exclude any other procedure, and this board of arbitration is not called upon to substitute its wisdom for that of the parties or to change or alter the terms of the agreement* [emphasis supplied].[2]

It is easy to see why the arbitrator ruled as he did. One of the basic contentions of the company was that the union representative had caused interference with production during his visits. For it to say this was not to establish it. In the absence of supporting evidence, the arbitrator was left with no alternative. Had the company provided some reasonable proof, the arbitrator might have found the union in violation of the provision prohibiting the business agent from work interference. His ruling would probably have been the same as it was, however. This most certainly would have been so in view of the significance of the company's attempting during negotiations to obtain conditions which it included in its unilateral rules of visitation.

Could a union president accompany a company industrial engineer and the union's international industrial engineer to a work site while a task was being time-studied? This was the question faced by Arbitrator J. K. Hayes. In accordance with the contract, the union requested an international industrial engineer be permitted entry to the plant to examine and study standards for a certain painter's job. Permission was granted by the company. However, as the two industrial engineers representing their respective parties were preparing to go to the job, the union requested that its local president (and chairman of the shop committee) accompany them to the job. The company denied this request and cited a contract clause:

> When a grievance involving the establishment or revision of a rate has been filed, the union may, if it desires, examine all the data which the company has pertaining to the dispute. A qualified industrial engineer of the International union may enter the plant to examine and study the opera-

tion involved at the conclusion of Step 3 of the grievance procedure. When such engineer is in the plant, he will at all times be accompanied by a representative of the company and the servicing International Representative of the union.

Following the company's refusal, the union stated that it would not go to the disputed job without the local union president, and the international representative departed from the plant. Subsequently, a grievance was filed, and at the arbitration hearing, the union cited the following contract provision in support of its position:

> In the event that it is necessary for an investigation of the facts by an employee representing the union in one of the steps of the grievance procedure, and such investigation must be made at a time when the employee interviewed is working in accordance with his regular schedule, or requires the investigator's absence from his scheduled work, permission must be obtained from the supervisor of the investigator and the employee to be interviewed before the interview may be made; such permission shall not be withheld unreasonably. If the supervisor is not available, permission must be obtained from the division superintendent.[3]

The position of the union was that the contract gave the union president a right to be present at the job. Second, it argued that past practice had been to allow the local chairman of the shop committee the right to go out on the job to investigate grievances. Third, it contended it was necessary for him to be present when a time study was being done so he might discuss such situations more clearly with management on other occasions; also, there might be various points on which the international representative would desire clarification from the local repesentative and vice versa.

The arbitrator concluded the company did violate the agreement when it refused to permit the union president to be present at a job to be time-studied by the international union industrial engineer. However, the arbiter specifically limited his award to this grievance and ruled that it should not be used as a precedent.

Upon a careful reading of the published decision, this finding is hard to square with the controlling contract language, which appears to be clear and unambiguous. Certainly it would have been in the best interests of both parties to make sure that the international representative who did the time study was a qualified industrial engineer. Any time study is a technical job to be done by someone with technical competence. Since both parties would be represented by technically competent individuals representing their respective interests, it surely seems superfluous for additional individuals to be present. This might have been the more sound conclusion in the face of contract language which clearly named the individual from the union authorized and empowered to be a part of such time-study proceedings.

A contract contained a clause stating that the union had the right to bring in "any representative of the union not an employee of the company" for the purpose of investigating grievances. Further, the contract provided that the employer "recognizes some grievances by their very nature may require investigation on the job." By virtue of such language, the union claimed a right to call in an international staff man to check the accuracy of incentive standards. The company's version of the problem was that the standard was designed to yield 20 percent over the basic rate, in accordance with the contract. The company commented it had provided the contractual opportunity for employees to achieve the 20 percent target. Hence, the question of whether an international staff man should have the right to study the incentive standards became irrelevant; but the question of a study would become relevant only if the employees lacked this opportunity of attaining the 20 percent level at standard performance. Furthermore, the employer insisted, bringing in an international staff man to time-study the operations would produce interventions which would be unreasonable and might lead to disclosure of various operations the company deemed secret for competitive reasons. Last but not least, it would interfere with the work of the employees while the time study was being made.

So far as the arbitrator was concerned, the company failed to demonstrate that the relevant employees clearly had the opportunity to obtain the 20 percent target. Secondly, there was no direct showing by the company that the work crew had been purposely holding back. Understandably, this rendered its argument that the grievance was irrelevant and nonarbitrable empty; so it was deemed an arbitrable issue. With contract language as clear and unequivocal as this, giving the union the right to bring in an international staff man (or "any representative of the union, not an employee of the company"), the only question remaining for the arbitrator was whether "grievance investigation" encompassed the right of an international staff man to make a time study of disputed standards.

In this connection, the contract language stating "the company recognizes that some grievances by their very nature may require *investigation on the job*" clearly implied, in the case of disputed incentive standards, that studies by an international staff were permissive, for how else could the staff man determine accurately whether the standards were proper?[4]

In another case, the union was ruled not entitled under a contract that contained an arbitration clause to have arbitration regarding its claim to right of access to the employees' cafeteria for the purpose of communicating with employees during their nonworking time. The compelling consideration for finding the matter not arbitrable was the arbitrator's interpretation that the labor agreement gave the right to seek the arbitration of grievances only to individual employees, not to the union.[5]

Such was not the case in a dispute between Hilton Hotels and the Hotel and Restaurant Employees and Bartenders International Union. The contract stated: "The union business agent, or his authorized representative, shall have the right to enter the employer's premises for business pertinent to this agreement, after first securing the approval of the manager or his representative. Such approval will not be unreasonably withheld." Article 3 of the agreement, entitled "Union Membership," included a standard union-shop provision requiring employees become members of the union within 31 days after they were first hired to remain members in good standing during their employment. Various union business representatives periodically contacted employees to collect union dues and to notify new hires of their duty to join the union.

Finally, management advised the union that the employees' cafeteria could not be used as a dues-collecting point and that such union business would have to be conducted at the foot of some stairs leading up to a watchman's station and time clock. The portion of the premises to which management gave the union access was a narrow area of cement sidewalk just a few feet in from the public sidewalk and immediately adjacent to the ramp where automobiles drove into the hotel. The area was covered by a roof but was open to the weather one one side. The union contended that the restriction placed on access to the premises for business representatives constituted a violation of the collective bargaining agreement.

In awarding the union the right at any time to enter the hotel and contact union members or new hires for business pertinent to the agreement, including the discussion of union membership and collection of dues, the arbitrator provided that such contacts should be made only during nonworking hours of employees. Second, such contacts should be made only in those locations in the hotel not generally open to the public, and such contacts should not interfere in any way with other employees of the hotel working at the time. The arbiter remarked:

> The opinion of the arbitrator, the limitations imposed upon access to the premises in this case constituted an unreasonable withholding of the right

to enter the employer's premises within the meaning and intent of Article 3. Restricting the business representative to a small area a few feet off the sidewalk, exposed to weather conditions, is clearly not necessary to protect the employer's legitimate interest in efficiency of the hotel's operation.[6]

The problem of access to a company's premises for union purposes most commonly arises in cases involving organizational attempts by unions. After a substantial amount of litigation in this area, the National Labor Relations Board and the courts established a general rule which permits the company latitude to establish reasonable rules against union activities during working hours. However, these laws do not allow the prohibition of such union activities during the time the employees are on nonworking, off-duty time, though they may still be on company premises.

The Supreme Court has approved this general rule, which it stated as follows:

> The act of course does not prevent an employer from making and enforcing reasonable rules covering the conduct of employees on company time. Working time is for work. It is therefore within the province of any employer to promulgate and enforce a rule prohibiting a union solicitation during working hours. Such a rule must be presumed to be valid in the absence of evidence that it was adopted for discriminatory purposes. It is no less true that time outside working hours, whether before or after work, or during luncheon or rest periods is an employee's time to use as he wishes without unreasonable restraint, although the employee is on company property.[7]

This is not to say that a union representative should have no latitude in pursuing their legitimate duties under an agreement. If both parties would sincerely address themselves to working out mutually acceptable visitation procedures and establishing agreed-upon boundaries for what is considered reasonable behavior on both sides, obviously the tensions which lead to disputes could be significantly minimized. But such an arrangement would certainly include the opportunity for each supervisor to know where each employee, including all stewards, was at all times and to make sure that all employees were at all times pursuing their regularly assigned duties in their duly designated areas within the institution. But it would also provide that supervisors are expected to permit reasonable contact between stewards and employees during working hours for the purpose of legitimate activities under the agreement, bearing in mind that such programs should be carried out in a minimum of time and without interfering with or disrupting the orderly procedures of work assignments.

The company should not interfere with the right of union representatives to carry on legitimate activities. Reasonable contract limitations are not those which prohibit union representatives from leaving their place of work at all. To maintain control and function in a manner equitable to all concerned, the company must preserve its right to exercise control over its personnel which is not in violation of the union's privileges or rights, as spelled out in the agreement. Where the agreement provides that employee–union representatives receive company payments while pursuing union duties, the company supervisors have a right to know where they are while they are being paid. Accordingly, the company needs the cooperation of the union in controlling the time spent by union representatives in processing grievances. And in a healthy and progressive relationship the union will cooperate in reducing to a minimum time spent in investigating, presenting, and adjusting grievances. It is with this expectation that the privilege of stewards to devote time during working hours to in-plant activities is granted – with the understanding that the time will be devoted to the prompt handling of legitimate grievances and will not be abused.

In a dispute decided by Arbitrator J. A. C. Grant between General Controls Company and the IAM, several issues concerning plant access were involved.[8] It was found that company rules requiring union business agents to give the personnel office a list of employees they wished to interview and to conduct interviews in a private office furnished by the company were violative of the contract's ban on company regulations which would render ineffective the contract's guarantee that union business agents might enter company property during working hours to carry out "necessary investigations of complaints and grievances." A rule requiring the business agent to inform the company of the specific grievance he wished to investigate was deemed proper, however. Although the contract permitted the business agent to enter the plant to investigate "complaints of working conditions" and might be construed to prohibit his entering the plant in the absence of any complaint, it was ruled that it could not be construed to prohibit his entering the plant to investigate complaints which had not yet been filed in writing. The grievance procedure clearly contemplated employees might have a grievance before they filed it in writing. It was further ruled the employer could properly insist that the union agent be accompanied by a company representative while going to and from the unit he desired to visit, but such employer representative could not remain near the union agent while he conversed with employees. Any listening in on such conversations or other prying into activities of the union agent were deemed a violation of the provisions of this contract.

Sometimes, rather than a question of whether the union generally has access to plant areas, the issue is whether access is prohibited in certain areas because of security problems it raises. Arbitrator Edgar A. Jones, Jr., had to resolve a grievance which raised that type of question between Librascope and the IAM. He found the employer had violated the contract's recognition clause when it denied union officials and stewards access to plant engineering departments and required the union to channel through the personnel manager inquiries whether engineering department employees, who were excluded from the bargaining unit by a decision of the National Labor Relations Board, were actually performing bargaining-unit work. He found that the grievance procedure permitted the union to initiate grievances on its own motion and thereby required that the union be allowed to investigate possible assignments of bargaining work to employees outside that unit.

Certain of his observations on this particular issue are interesting and may provide guidance in cases of this type:

> Were the union to be foreclosed the grievance procedure unless and until a member-employee duly filed a grievance the restrictions upon union entry into plant areas would require a closer degree of scrutiny of particular phrasing in the collective bargaining agreement correlated with the precise procedures imposed by the Company as conditions to entry of union representatives, than is true in this case. *Under that type of grievance procedure the grievance comes to the union for processing.* The union need only secure *that degree* of access to plant areas which will allow it fairly to respond to the call of its aggrieved member. The case here, however, is different. Here the union is empowered to generate a grievance on its own motion "with respect to fulfillment of its obligations under the terms of the Agreement.". . .
>
> A restriction which keeps a union steward at his work station unless his ear is sought by a potentially aggrieved employee may be valid *where the Agreement does not* contain a provision like Sec. F of Art. XI empowering the union to institute a grievance itself. A restriction which requires the union representative to divulge to a company representative the nature of details of a putative grievance he seeks to investigate preparatory to a decision by the union whether or not to institute its own grievance against the company is an improper intrusion into the operation of [this] grievance procedure.
>
> This does *not* mean that the Company cannot under the Agreement take steps to comply with security regulations whether those of and pertaining to the Defense Department or to the Company's own competitively intended product development. . . . It is regrettable that union investigation of putative grievances may interfere with the smooth operation of work

procedures or make more difficult the application of security cautions. But this is one of the prices the parties have undertaken to pay for nonviolent dispute settlement through the establishment of a collective bargained grievance procedure. The strike and the lockout are the alternative rejected by the parties [emphasis added].[9]

In addition, the arbitrator made it clear that arrangements could be made to avoid any breach of security regulations pertaining to legitimate Engineering Department work.

Last but not least is one decided by Vernon L. Stouffer for Avco Mfg. and the IBEW. It was ruled the employer did not violate the contract by refusing to grant a departmental steward permission to go into another department to see whether engineering department employees were doing bargaining-unit work. In this matter the decision turned on the contract language, which in this instance was more restrictive. The contract restricted stewards to handling grievances of employees in their assigned department, and authorization to leave "his place of work" to investigate such grievances did not contemplate his leaving the department. Moreover, the contract confined the rights and privileges of stewards to situations where a grievance or a dispute *already existed* and did not give them the right to go into other departments or areas seeking to determine if there were contract violations. Arbitrator Stouffer's decision stated:

> The Chairman has carefully examined Article IX, Section 3, and other Articles and Sections of the currently effective Agreement, most of which are set forth above, and is constrained to find that the investigative rights and privileges of stewards are confined to situations where a grievance or dispute already exists. Stewards do *not* have the right to go into Departments and areas other than the ones to which they are assigned, seeking possible or potential violations of the Collective Bargaining Agreement. To permit this would undoubtedly create an intolerable situation. The inherent right of the union to police the Agreement does not extend this far.[10]

Comparing these last two cases, the dissimilarities between the two cases was in contract language, and it was around this governing and essential factor that each case turned and was decided. Before any judgment is made regarding the union's right of access and the extent of it, the manager should carefully scrutinize his labor agreement, examining all its relevant provisions and relating them to the essence of the cases cited herein. This may provide a general direction in any situation.

The denial of access to company premises for union representatives may also be based upon the prior behavior and conduct of the union official. Such behavior may have been sufficiently provocative and troublesome on prior occasions for the company to consider his presence undesirable. An employer has been held not to have violated a contract which guaranteed union representatives access to the plant when it refused admittance to a union representative who had created an air of intimidation and threatened use of force against the company's president during a prior grievance discussion. The arbitrator found that the representative's conduct had been overly aggressive and threatening to the personal well-being of the official. Significant was his conclusion that this representative was knowledgeable, skillful, and well trained. He was not an unsophisticated, uninformed, or uneducated shop worker who might under certain circumstances have been excused for an uncontrolled emotional outburst under pressure. The arbitrator believed that his conduct had been calculated and intended to create intimidation. Under these circumstances, the arbitrator denied the union's grievance and found the company's action justified.[11]

While custom and practice are frequently used to establish the intent of contract provisions which are ambiguous, custom and practice ordinarily will not be used to give meaning to a provision which is clear and unambiguous.[12] Where the contract language is manifestly unambiguous, practices which may have varied with that language usually become immaterial, and many arbitrators have held that a meaning suggested by practice other than that expressed will not compromise language which is clear.

Such was the case in a dispute between the Associated Hospitals of the Eastbay and the Hospital and Institutional Workers Union. Here the contract permitted union representatives to visit the employer's hospital to determine whether the agreement was being carried out. Such permission was extended as long as the visiting privilege was "exercised reasonably," the union representative reported "to a designated management official when entering," and did not "interfere with the normal conduct of work." An arbitrator decided the employer could not require the representative to specify the reason for a visit in advance, to make appointments for visits, or to permit hospital officials to escort him during his visit. This was his finding notwithstanding the company's contention that these practices had been established by the past practice of the parties since the contract was clear and unambiguous; therefore, the past practice of the parties inconsistent with the contract could not change its meaning. However, he would allow management to retain its right to revoke a representative's hospital institution privileges if he acted unreasonably during the visit or if there was a legitimate reason for believing in advance that he would act unreasonably during such a visit.[13]

Another grievance arose when management at first refused to permit a shop steward to enter its laboratory to investigate whether any bargaining unit work was being performed there but later allowed him to enter. In this case it was established that in the course of their work several members of the bargaining unit went in and out of the laboratory. It also was established that there was nothing secret about the work performed in the laboratory. The agreement permitted the steward to leave his department to investigate a grievance. In settlement of the grievance protesting the employer's delay, the following procedures suggested by the employer at the hearing were approved:

1. The chief steward or committeeman were enabled to request permission of their supervisor to go to the employee relations department from which he would be conducted immediately, unannounced, to the area in question to conduct his investigation; or
2. These same union representatives might request their supervisor to arrange a meeting for him with the supervisor of the area he wished to investigate.[14]

Access to Data

Since 1956 the courts and the National Labor Relations Board have legislated extensions of earlier rulings in this "informational" area of the act, which in substance require that the employer is obligated to supply such economic data and information in a manner "sufficient to enable the Union to bargain intelligently." Such material is further intended to enable the union to understand and discuss issues raised by an employer which are in opposition to union demands and enable it to administer the contract.[15] Concepts such as these continue to be applicable rules of law by later affirmations in the courts and by the board.[16] As these concepts have evolved over the years, it has been determined that this "employer duty" is not necessarily restricted to a period of contract negotiations between the parties. Such duty has been construed to continue beyond the negotiation period into the administrative life of the agreement. This concept is intended to allow the union to administer its agreement more intelligently and effectively. The board ruled that "8(a)5 [of the act] imposes an obligation to furnish all information relevant to the bargaining representative's intelligent performance of its function. This obligation extends to information which the Union may require in order to police and administer existing agreements."[17]

For the employer to offer the desired and requested information at arbitration but withhold it beforehand does not satisfy its duty. The board has said, "It is no answer to a request for information to state that the information will be forthcoming in the course of an arbitration proceeding. To sustain this would put the employer in the position to force the union to arbitration, (and the expense connected), even in those instances where had the union had the information, it would have determined that the grievances were without merit."[18]

During the administrative periods of the contract, the most prevalent union request for information is in the area of time studies. In this connection, the board has held that not only are time studies required to be furnished to the union for its bargaining purposes but also that the employer must permit the union to have access to the plant to enable it to make its own time studies of the disputed operations in pending grievances.[19]

However, such decisions appear to have a thread of commonality – further requiring that the information sought by the union be relevant to its task as a bargaining agent either in negotiating the contract or adjusting a grievance which may fall within the contractual purview.

In a case involving Hercules Motor Corp. the union filed a grievance regarding the fairness of certain incentive standards rates.[20] The union asked to examine the employer's data related to the disputed operations, also asking for an opportunity to make its own time study. These requests were refused by the company on the argument that the agreement did not give the right to the union to dispute the fairness of rates. The employer did indicate to the union that if this matter was found to be grievable by an arbitrator, it would then, but not until then, supply the requested information. The union chose to file 8(a)(5) charges with the NLRB. However, the board held that this was an issue of contract interpretation and therefore not properly before the board. This was not the simple case of a union seeking and being denied information *pertinent and relevant* to its role as a bargaining agent. In this instance the union was seeking information to support a grievance dealing with a matter which the company (perhaps properly) contended could not be the valid subject matter for a grievance. It may also be held that the employer need not furnish information which the union can reasonably obtain from other convenient sources or from information it already has.[21]

In cases involving charges of violation of the National Labor Relations Act, it has been held even in cases where there was no contract provision to aid the union that

1. An employer is required to furnish a union on request with sufficient data on wages and allied matters.[22]

2. This requirement includes original data on time studies.[23]
3. The data must be furnished for the processing of grievances as well as for general collective bargaining.[24]
4. As to relevance, it is sufficient if the information sought is "related" to the issue.[25]
5. Such data must be supplied even though the employer considers it confidential.[26]

The Teamsters Union brought a refusal-to-bargain charge against an employer who refused either to furnish the union with data pertaining to overtime worked in a five-month period by union employees and also worked by employees of the employer's subcontractor or to give the union access to the data in question. The board found that this employer violated the LMRA since the information sought by the union was relevant to pending grievances which were concerned with the method of assigning overtime under the agreement. Influencing the board's reasoning was the fact that the company did not contend the information sought by the union covered too great a period of time or would impose too great a burden. It merely questioned the relevance of the information and claimed the company had satisfied its obligation.

The company also contended that the subcontractor's employees had worked overtime that should have been assigned to unit employees and that such unit employees had worked an excessive number of hours during the week and therefore were physically unable to work overtime on the weekend. But by having asserted physical incapacity as a basis for denying the grievances, the employer was obliged to supply all relevant data in support of that assertion. In this context, the information sought by the union was relevant, material, and necessary to enable it to decide whether the grievances should be dropped or past overtime assignment practices cast sufficient doubt on the company's justification. The problem presented by the grievances was sufficiently recurrent to warrant its proceeding to arbitration.[27]

Without dwelling on a number of board cases involving the issue of access to information, an examination of a single case reveals the direction the board's thinking takes on disputes like this – *General Electric Company case v. NLRB,* which was appealed by this employer in the U.S. Fourth Circuit Court of Appeals where the board's decision was upheld.

General Electric operated a plant where it manufactured distribution transformers. One of the tasks performed by workmen was that of coil winding on jobs subject to production standards established by time studies made pursuant to a General Electric system known as motion time study (MTS). This type of system involves the use of predetermined time values for certain body motions and movements. A number of grievances raised questions such as whether the MTS system applicable to a certain operation was being improperly used for another operation, whether insufficient time allowances were provided for various coil winding operations, whether the removal of a particular employee from his coil-winding job was without just cause based on the union's premise that the time standards were incorrect, and whether certain disciplinary notices given to employees by the company for consistent failures to meet standards were unjustified based on the premise that time studies were inaccurate.

The union contended it should be allowed to have one of its time-study engineers make his own studies on the job. Further, he should be on the scene whenever time studies were made by General Electric. The company did offer to allow the union (but not its time-study engineer expert) to examine the company's time study rate, but it steadfastly refused to permit the union's time-study engineer to conduct independent time studies of production standards. While it did permit them to examine motion pictures of the company's retiming of certain disputed production standards, it would not permit the union's time-study engineer to be present when the company's professional retimed disputed production standards. Unilaterally and voluntarily, the company did review the disputed time standards and in some cases increased time allowances. The union's argument was that it could not intelligently represent its members without independent data. General Electric contended that the setting of production standards was a prerogative and a responsibility of the company, that the presence of the union's time-study engineer during retiming of disputed standards would have an interruptive and disruptive influence, and that all data it was willing to make available to the union was sufficient to enable the union to determine if the MTS system had been correctly developed and properly applied.

The board's trial examiner determined that the union was entitled as a matter of statutory right to the information it requested in the manner the union demanded. However, he ruled the union had waived its right to have its time-study engineer conduct independent time studies of production standards involved in the grievance and the right to conduct independent evaluation of jobs by personal observation. The board affirmed the trial examiner with regard to the right of the union's time-study engineer to inspect General Electric time-study data. However, the board reversed him on the issues of independent time studies and evaluations by personal observation. The board's conclusion in this regard was that the union had not waived its rights by the collective bargaining agreement.

The Fourth Circuit Court of Appeals decision went like this:

> We think that there was substantial evidence to support the finding that
> in order intelligently to participate in the grievance procedures established
> by the contract, the union should be given the opportunity to conduct in-
> dependent time studies of production standards, for its expert to inspect
> General Electric time study data, and have its expert conduct independent
> evaluations by personal observation.

The court cited *Fafnir Bearing Co. v. the NLRB* where the company
had provided the union's time-study engineer its time-study information
but had refused to allow the union to conduct "live" studies for a union
evaluation of the company's proposed incentive standards.[28]

Last but certainly not least in the considerations by the court were
its remarks relative to the contract's "zipper" clause. Here, the court
departed from respectable principles of industrial relations and contract
construction. With regard to the weight and impact of this contractual
provision on the issue, the court remarked:

> Finally, we find no waiver in the "wrap up" clause of the contract, which
> recited that it and related documents constituted full settlement of all
> issues which were the subject matter of collective bargaining between the
> parties and, as a result, that each of the parties agreed that none of such
> issues shall be subject to collective bargaining during the term of the con-
> tract. This provision merely purports to excuse, during the term of the con-
> tract, each party from any statutory duty to comply with the other's re-
> quest to enter into negotiations with respect to any such issue about which
> the parties had bargained in pre-contract negotiations. This provision left
> the parties respective rights to demand or refuse grievance data to the re-
> maining provisions of the contract, which we have concluded did not affec-
> tively waive the union's statutory rights to such data.[29]

In its decision the Court was influenced by the strong public policy
to make the grievance procedure established by the parties the means for
accomplishing industrial peace, on the premise that access to such information to make both parties fully effective was in the best interests of
an enlightened employer as well as the union. On the court's and the
Board's appraisal of the "zipper" clause, it would require a substantial in-
jection of logic plasma to make it any more than the anemic opinion it is
viewed to be by most industrial-relations professionals.

Another question revolved around merit increases given by an
employer solely at its discretion, based on a company contention that
such wage increases were not a legitimate concern of the union under the

labor contract. The parties entered an agreement, the first between them, which did not contain a union-shop provision but did provide for maintenance of membership by those employees who would join the union. It also provided that wage increases would be automatic up to midpoint of each labor grade but that after the midpoint, each employee was to receive increases, "provided his performance merits it." The origin of the complaint came from two men working together who received disparate rates of pay. When questioned by a union official, the company explained the reasons for the difference. Growing out of this discussion came a union request for a list of all unit employees and their rates of pay. The employer submitted a list which included pay rates for employees at the midpoint of the labor grades and below, but the list contained only the names of employees above the midpoint, not their labor rates.

Of a total of 178 employees listed, 142 were above midpoint. A union representative then wrote to the company asking for rates of pay and classifications of all unit employees, contending this was necessary to check the company's compliance with the contract clause covering wage rates and wage increases. The company forwarded a copy of the same material previously furnished. In reply to this, the union asserted that the information furnished by the company was not sufficiently explicit and expressed a belief that the employer was discriminating between employees who belonged to the union and those who did not. The union then requested the "actual wage rates" of *all* employees, along with their classifications. The employer refused on the premise that the company did not consider the information sought a matter of legitimate union concern. This was based on its contention that rates above the midpoint were based on merit and within the company's sole discretion. The company further reminded the union that it had been supplied with individual wage rates during the past contract negotiations and that no current negotiations regarding wage rates were in progress. The union elected to file a charge with the board and did not pursue the matter through the formal grievance procedure.

The board considered two contractual provisions relevant. First, Article 3, the management clause, provided that "nothing herein will be used to discriminate against any employee because of his union membership." Another contract clause provided that an employee would receive an increase beyond the midpoint of the salary range "provided his performance merits it." With reference to this provision, the parties stipulated that it was "entirely discretionary whether or not they [company] gave merit increases above the mid-point range."

Under such language, the board ruled that the union had not waived

its right to the requested information or its right to file a grievance if it
felt the employer was discriminating on the basis of union membership
in awarding merit increases. Second, the union's right to the requested
information derived from the act and not from the agreement. Third, the
wage information the union requested was presumptively relevant to the
union's obligation as the employees' bargaining representative. Four, the
employer failed to show good cause justifying its refusal to supply the requested information.[30]

The union's request for information may be motivated by its desire
to use the requested information to further its organizational efforts.
This was the nature of the dispute decided by the board between parties
who had experienced a bargaining relationship since 1945. The employer
had 2,600 employees, with about 1,770 represented by the union throughout five counties of southern California. Over the years, the principal
issue between the parties had been that of union security, with the union
unable to gain such a clause in bargaining. Because of this failure, it had
attempted unsuccessfully on many occasions to obtain from the company
the addresses of employees in the unit, admittedly to be used for organizational purposes. The company had consistently declined to provide the
information: to do so would invade employees' rights to privacy. During
recent negotiations one of the union's proposals had been a demand for
names and addresses of all employees. However, no agreement was
reached on this point. The contract remained silent, and negotiations
were ultimately consummated by a new agreement. A few months into
the new contract, the union again made a claim for the information, contending it was necessary to administer the contact. The board's ruling
was that the employer had violated the Labor Management Relations
Act by refusing to comply with this union request, in view of the board's
prior decisions in a Standard Oil Company case and Prudential Insurance
Company case.[31]

The above-cited cases may bring light into this clouded area of labor-
management relations. They may also alert management to the danger
inherent in arbitrary refusals of information requested by the union.
Perhaps the safest general rule of thumb should be for management to
consider carefully any request for data actually needed by the union to
understand, prepare, or present facts and positions on any dispute which
deals with a matter covered by a provision of the agreement and if
reasonable and proper using that basic criteria, to grant it to the extent
required to satisfy it reasonably.

Chapter 5
Union Latitude
in Grievance Handling

Offensive Language and Abusive Behavior

It is conceded a shop steward should be able to represent his members zealously and while acting in the capacity of a union representative be permitted a certain latitude in behavior and enjoy a certain immunity from discipline. The handling of a grievance between the union's steward and the foreman is basically an adversary situation, and each party is expected to represent vigorously the interests of its organization.

How far can a union representative go in representing the interests of his constituents and defending what he believes to be legitimate rights of his union? How much of an altercation, if any, may be tolerable between a union official and a representative of management? No black or white answers are available to questions such as these, but how disputes involving these questions are answered by arbitrators may provide some interesting insights. Two union officials were discharged for misconduct including a physical altercation with the shop superintendent. Immediately prior to the incident, which culminated in discharge, the superintendent had observed an employee distributing leaflets to employees without having obtained approval. Suspending the employee, the superintendent accompanied him to the time-clock area. Here the superintendent noticed a pile of the same leaflets inside the timekeeper's office. He took possession of these and started to walk to the plant manager's office to advise him of the situations he had experienced.

The labor agreement between the parties contained a prohibition on distribution of leaflets in the absence of written approval: "The union agrees that there will be no distribution of handbills or other union materials on company time or property, except if such notices or materials have been approved in writing by the Director of Industrial Relations or his designated representative."

On his way to the plant manager's office, the superintendent encountered another union official, who demanded return of the leaflets, claiming they were union property and challenging the superintendent's right to have them in his possession. The superintendent refused to hand them over, whereupon the first union official proceeded to engage him in a scuffle, attempting to recover the leaflets. The superintendent managed to resist, but during the altercation another union steward joined with the first official, and the handbills were wrested from the superintendent. Much of this physical dispute was witnessed by several second-shift employees coming through the area, who were attracted by the shouting and commotion.

Upon being given suspension notices and ordered to leave the plant, the two union officials remained on the premises protesting their suspension and beseeching incoming employees not to enter the plant on the premise that they would be without union representation. The plant manager was summoned and summarily ordered the grievants to leave, finally finding it necessary to summon plant guards and local police.

The arbitrator's appraisal of the matter is significant:

> Although an argument could be advanced that [the superintendent] may have used questionable judgment under the circumstances, and even may have provoked the anger of the two employees involved, these circumstances would neither excuse nor justify the actions which followed. Even assuming that [superintendent] had no right to confiscate or impound the circulars, at the most his conduct would have given rise to a grievance which could have adequately been handled through the grievance procedure including arbitration. In no event did his actions justify resorting to selfhelp and physical force to rectify or prevent a threatened wrong. Any other holding would make of the contract and grievance procedure a "fair weather" utility to be disregarded under circumstances of industrial stress. The terms of the contract were written and intended to govern the relations between the parties and the preamble proclaims that both the company, the union and its representatives and employees shall be bound by its provisions.
>
> It should be observed that what was here involved was an attempt by two employees to forcefully wrest from a superintendent a quantity of circulars and which involved a tussle lasting "a minute or more" and in which considerable tugging and pulling took place. While it is not claimed that either of the grievants struck the [superintendent] or incidated any intention to do him physical harm, the instant in and of itself may have had serious consequences of personal injury to the participant. That such did not occur may be attributed to the good judgment of [superintendent] in finally giving up the struggle and relinquishing the contested leaflets.[1]

The arbitrator's conclusions were notwithstanding the union's claim that the circulars were not being distributed at the time of the seizures. He further discounted that the superintendent had no authority to confiscate leaflets which were the property of the union. Also given no consideration was the union's argument that the physical force exerted by their representatives was directed solely to retrieving the circulars and was not accompanied by any physical violence against the superintendent's person. The only relevant point was that in so conducting themselves they were guilty of an inexcusable impropriety and subjected themselves to discipline.

Management should not forget that a union representative does have a responsibility for assertively representing union members and pursuing grievances submitted by them. The fact is that the very qualities of aggressiveness, directness, bluntness, and the like may have been those which enamored an elected representative to his membership and convinced them he would effectively defend and represent their interests. Contrasting the union steward and his objectives with those of a management representative, a supervisor carries a responsibility for maintaining discipline in his department and operating it as efficiently as possible. It is these varying functions which can produce strong differences of opinion, accompanied by emotion on the part of the respective advocates. It should be expected that union representatives will undertake the pursuit of grievances in a vigorous fashion and present viewpoints in a positive, assertive fashion. However, there is a line which must be drawn between the use of mere shoptalk or repartee and the use of vile language and behavior which is contemptuous and disrespectful. The line between being abusive and being merely argumentative may well be influenced by a tone of voice which is insulting.

Arbitrator Maurice S. Trotta made this point in a clear and definite way in one of his opinions when he remarked, "A distinction must be drawn, however, between presenting arguments in a positive manner and being argumentative. There is a difference between attacking the logic of a decision and attacking the man who made the decision. Moreover, we cannot ignore tone of voice or attitude. These may be just as important as the words used."[2] He made these comments when sustaining the discipline of a union steward for abusive remarks to his foreman when the supervisor told him of another employee's earlier request for a conference with the steward. Although the manager conceded that stewards are expected to present arguments in a positive manner, he believed the steward's behavior tended to aggravate the problem. The steward presented the foreman with a grievance protesting alleged disregard of the employee's right to representation immediately instead of first finding out why a meeting had not been arranged. The employee's grievance was not urgent, and the request for the meeting with the steward had been made just a short time before. The steward had been out of the department at the time of the request and not available for the meeting and the steward told the foreman that the meeting had already been held without indicating that it had been held during the lunch period, not on company time, in circumvention of the usual procedure.

Even though it may be proved that a union representative had been belligerent and used profane language with his foreman, a penalty imposed for such conduct may be mitigated by extenuating circumstances. A union president was discharged for "insubordination and threatening and belligerent conduct directed at his supervisor" after a dispute over maintenance work the union president-operator thought was being done without required work orders. The evidence seemed clear that the union official was guilty of using profane and abusive language toward the supervisor. However, the company did not supply sufficient evidence to show that he made any physical threat toward the maintenance supervisor.

Finding him guilty of using profane and abusive language directed at the supervisor, the arbitrator held that a disciplinary penalty was appropriate. The question was whether discharge was the appropriate remedy. Significant to this case was the fact that the company had discharged the individual based at least in part on a contention that he was *also* insubordinate. On this claim the company could provide no proof. Although his attitude and remarks and belligerence left much to be desired and merited discipline, he was not guilty of insubordinate action. As the arbitrator stated on this point, "An essential element of the offense of insubordination consists of either refusing to perform or carry out orders given the employee by a supervisor with proper authority, or taking some action that the employee is instructed not to do. There is no evidence to show that the grievant disobeyed any orders or instructions given him."[3]

The grievant had 11 years of service with the company with his work regarded as satisfactory and no prior formal discipline on his record. The arbitrator reinstated the grievant without an award of back pay between the time of his discharge and the date of his reinstatement. Because of this period, it made it plain to the grievant that this was a serious penalty in keeping with the seriousness of the offense of using profane and abusive language to a management member.

A warning issued to a shop steward by the company for accusing management of "thieving and robbery" in a grievance discussion with the foreman over the application of an incentive standard was ordered withdrawn by an arbitrator. To allow this disciplinary notice to stand would have appeared to establish a precedent that could have been harder for the parties to live with than the possibility that occasionally a loudmouthed shop steward might overstep the bounds of orderliness and decorum. In rendering such an award for the union, the arbitrator by no means intended to suggest that any and all conduct, activity, or expressions of shop stewards during grievance meetings were clothed with immunity from plant discipline. To the contrary, he made it emphatically clear to the steward that his expression in this instance was improper and damaging to the relations between the parties.[4]

A union officer was suspended for three days after having an initial discussion with the superintendent concerning a time standard on a production line, as provided in the contract's grievance procedure, then took matters into his own hands and engaged in a heated discussion with the superintendent, during which he used an obscene remark. Although the parties could not agree upon the actual remark made by the union officer, the arbitrator dealt with the matter in the following way:

> The use of so-called "shop language" is common in every day relations between industrial employees and at times the expressions used go well beyond the limits generally accepted in polite conversation. In the rugged environment of a punch press production line operated with the accompanying noise and tensions, no one would endeavor to stop completely the use of profanity in any form. There are, however, degrees of this shop language. *Profanity,* while of little value in informing or impressing orders, is generally accepted. *Vulgarity,* the next level below profanity, tends to breed disrespect toward the user but is, again, generally tolerated, except when directed at another with malice. The third and lowest form, *obscenity,* should be "out of limits" at all times. When directed at a fellow employee, it inevitably leads to ill feeling and not infrequently to dissension destructive of efficiency. When directed at a Supervisor, it is completely beyond the limits of tolerance, it is tantamount to insubordination; it tends to replace reason with emotion and cooperation with opposition. Unrestricted use of vulgar and obscene language will lower the morale of a group with accompanying adverse effects on quality and efficiency. The manager who permits such language to be directed at his supervision – those placed in responsible charge of the men and equipment – is destined to find the establishment he is managing in deep trouble. No small part of his managerial talents must be directed to establishing high morale, confidence, and respect between workers and supervisors. He may encourage them to be *friendly* but he must insist on *respect.* Exchanges of vulgar language lessens the chances of success; obscenity precludes it.

> In the interchange of charges and countercharges, the parties to this

dispute have gone to considerable lengths to establish whether this grievant called the superintendent an obscene name or whether he used the
obscene term in a less direct reference to the position occupied by the
superintendent. The contentions of the parties on this point is a standoff.
In the judgment of this Arbitrator, however, the difference between the admission of the grievant prevails, it is unquestioned that the grievant
directed a vicious epithet at the stand taken by the Superintendent personally (as contended by the Company) or directed at the position which he
occupied and the results obtained when he performed the duties of that
position (as alleged by the Union). Either is unexcusable.[5]

Also significant to this dispute was that the union officer made his
original outburst in front of several others, while a subsequent apology
was made in private. However, his prompt and unsolicited apology did
show he recognized his error and the need for fair play. In view of this
fact and his prior unblemished record of four years the company
mitigated his penalty from a threatened discharge to a three-day unpaid
suspension from work. The arbitrator upheld this action.

Management's treatment of a union representative, at least so far as
its being upheld is concerned, may be influenced by the atmosphere and
environment of the overall labor-management relationship between the
parties. Although a union steward overstepped the bounds of "reasonable propriety" when he accused the company president of "paying off"
the previous union steward, his misconduct did not warrant the extreme
penalty of discharge. The employee was awarded reinstatement with full
seniority rights but without back pay for one month. Pertinent here was
that the dispute occurred against the background of several months of
unwholesome union-management relations in an apparent background
of intemperate, sarcastic, and abusive language which both parties had
resorted to. The arbitrator made it clear to the union steward and his
superior union officers that he would conduct himself with decorum and
a respectful attitude toward management representatives whatever the
real or fancied provocation he might feel.

Because management has condoned misconduct by a union representative in the past does not mean it must continue to excuse or overlook
actions for which disciplinary punishment might otherwise be appropriate. It seems to be a well-established principle of labor arbitration
that condonation is set aside by a later action of the same nature. Arbitrator B. Luskin stated this principle:

> The connotation of an offense does not require that the offense be con-
> sidered to have been forgiven for all time. Any subsequent offense similar
> in nature to one which was allegedly condoned serves to revive the original

offense. Stated as a simple form of principle, a condonation is effective only so long as the offender refrains from committing a similar type of offense. A repetition, in effect, revives the offense or offenses which were alleged to have been condoned.[6]

In most plants the parties get accustomed to the use of shoptalk, which often includes a good deal of profanity. In some situations the use of it is frequent and general and unfortunately is often not limited to hourly employees but is also used by members of supervision. On occasion this profanity may be used not in jest and thereby gives rise to anger and resentment. Place those ingredients into a situation where a union representative is eager in his championing of the rights of the union member and combining it with aggressive supervisors who are zealous in their representation of management interests, and you have the makings for a volatile experience.

These were factors which led to "a personality conflict between an emotional, aggressive but inexperienced shop steward . . . and an equally aggressive and experienced foreman, all of which resulted in turmoil and heated situations – one crisis after another." The employer in this case was held not justified in suspending a union representative who allegedly called his foreman a vulgar name. Arm waving was done by the foreman as well as the grievant, and the testimony demonstrated the foreman had also engaged in some name-calling.[7]

The union's usual arguments in disputes such as these is that throughout the course of the events, its representative was acting as a union official rather than as an employee and was accountable for his conduct not to the company but solely to the union. Such was the substance of the union's argument where a union steward was discharged for approaching a foreman and angrily threatening him with bodily harm for the company's failure to provide relief for his work gang. The steward here was not considered on union business for which he could not be disciplined since his immediate foreman had refused to excuse him from working 15 minutes before the end of the shift to present a grievance protesting the failure to provide relief. Instead, he had been docked for the remaining time on his shift and sent home as a disciplinary measure for his refusal to return to work. Taken together with his "extraordinarily bad" past disciplinary record, his outburst on this occasion was considered sufficient to justify discharge.[8]

None of this is intended to convey the impression that a union representative must be limited to language on the level of parlor talk. Nor does mere zealousness and militancy justify discipline. Clearly, the union representative's right to perform his job with a reasonable degree of freedom from fear of retaliation must be preserved. Some allowance must be given for this factor. Additional allowance must be made when shoptalk is employed, which is common in content to that customarily experienced by employees, union representatives, and supervisors in the work place. But the vernacular of the shop need not be countenanced or tolerated when it's carried into the company's general offices and occurs in the presence of women. These were the elements in a case where a 10-day disciplinary suspension was imposed on a union committeeman for insubordination and the use of profane language. Although the company charged the union official with ordering employees to stop working on a project to which they had been assigned by the company, there was not sufficient evidence to support this allegation. However, when he carried his complaint into the general offices to speak to the vice president of personnel in front of women clerical employees and engaged in the use of boisterous, coarse, and profane language, he was clearly in need of corrective discipline. This behavior cost him a three-day suspension and was deemed appropriate by an arbitrator.[9]

In the atmosphere of a church social, behavior sanctioned in the industrial work situation might well be objectionable and offensive. The typical industrial factory is certainly not a church social; language is often rough and manners frequently earthy. Therefore, when arbitrators are evaluating case circumstances, they must measure what is common and accepted in the particular workplace where the dispute occurs and not measure it against what is acceptable behavior in more-sheltered environments. And while management cannot select particular employees to serve as union representatives, neither can the union select management's representatives. Management, and the union for that matter, has every right to demand of the other side that whoever is chosen to handle its labor relations affairs be willing and able to function in a dignified and civil manner.

One dispute came before Arbitrator Joseph M. Klamon involving a union official who had been discharged twice. This novel situation resulted when a union official was discharged for using abusive and obscene language to his supervisor but in accordance with an agreement between the company and the union, was reinstated on the contention that he give up his duties as a union official. The parties signed this agreement, and the individual was reinstated but subsequently refused to comply with a reasonable order of his supervisor and also failed to give up his position in the union, continuing to function in the capacity of a union official. The employer discharged him again. His continued disobedience after reinstatement against the background of repeated warnings and his discharge for his insubordinate attitude "indicated little effort on the part of the grievant to accept reasonable orders or instructions of supervisors" in the judgment of the arbitrator.[10]

A variety of mitigating circumstances may influence the outcome where this type of issue is involved. A host of these influenced the conclusion of an arbitrator in a case with Bucyrus-Erie Company and the United Steelworkers. The employer had imposed a three-day disciplinary suspension upon a union committeeman who upon presenting grievances to his foreman on a strike deadline day, became involved in a dispute over the grievance procedure and advised his supervisor that in his opinion he had no welding ability and no education. The factors influencing the decision were the following:

1. There was no prior background of hostility between this foreman and this committeeman.
2. The committeeman was not scheduled to work that day or evening and was at that particular time being paid by the union.
3. He had put in a long day which had started at 4:00 A.M., and he was in a fatigued condition.
4. There was an air of tension in the plant created by the imminent strike deadline.
5. The discussion between the two advocates occurred in an office, not in a general work area, and was witnessed by just one other employee.
6. The committeeman did not usually work under any of the foremen who were present.
7. Certain remarks made by the welding foreman could have been construed as provocative.
8. The foreman to some extent participated in the discussion and condoned it by so doing.

Under these circumstances, the union official's language was not considered an affront to managerial authority, or having an adverse effect on production or any other interests of management.

Although this may be considered a minority viewpoint, it is an expression of a responsible and seasoned arbiter. Referred to is his conclusion that discipline would not be justified solely on the basis of the employee's insulting remarks to the foreman. For discipline to be upheld by the arbiter here, there had to be a showing that under these circumstances, the union officer's remarks adversely affected production or constituted a material affront to managerial authority.[11]

Ordinarily, the union representative is not subject to discipline by management when acting in his role as a union steward or officer, participating in a formal grievance discussion or similar union activity, and not functioning in his status as an employee. However, though the union steward is entitled to certain special privileges in pursuing grievances, he is not totally immunized from reprimand or discipline by virtue of his union office. Conceding such immunity could lead to an irresponsible undermining of the good-faith processing of grievances and generally to a deterioration of labor relations.

How much latitude should be allowed? The question in such cases always involves an interesting and delicate point of principle in the conduct of union-management relations. It would take volumes to examine and review thoroughly this issue and come out with satisfactory generalization which would fit all cases. The collective-bargaining relationship is such that there are frequent situations which are enormously complex and charged with intense emotions. There are times when the company or the union representatives act improperly as representatives or in their relationships to each other. The need of the parties to maintain the integrity and efficiency of the collective-bargaining machinery can normally be relied upon to ensure they will take proper steps to prevent the occurrence or improper actions by their representatives.

Although union representatives should be permitted a certain latitude in the presentation of their grievances, they must not be allowed to abuse or demean management personnel. An overly aggressive or emotional union steward may attempt to do just that, by threat or intimidation, to convert the foreman to his way of thinking. Language which exceeds the normal shop vernacular – shouting and other kinds of emotional conduct or expression by a union official, even while on proper union business – is not a condition management is obliged to endure. When such an atmosphere develops, management's representative should at least take steps to adjourn the discussion until the union representative is in a better frame of mind to discuss it. Under certain circumstances, the steward's behavior or remarks may be sufficiently provocative, demonstrative, violent, or disruptive for some form of disciplinary action.

But in labor-management relations there is no room for prejudice toward union representatives. The presence of the union organization in the plant brings about a union-management marriage producing a corresponding obligation to observe the vows of recognition and good faith. In their grievance relationship, the foreman and the steward are equals. The foreman and the steward are subject to similar pressures. The steward is expected to be apprised of plant rules, bonus systems, safety regulations, time-study matters, job-evaluation plans, pension plans, labor-law developments, and procedures of discipline. The foreman, because of his close relationship with the workers and their problems feels a closeness and a kinship with the workers which most other management representatives do not share. As a member of management, and as its spokesman and advocate, he may sometimes find himself in conflict with his personal feelings toward the issue. The steward faces a similar problem. His close association with the employees subjects him to certain group pressures and thinking which he as an individual and an employee may not personally support.

All of these factors are present when these two advocates come together. Each has a job to do and should be performing it in the manner which best serves the interests of his institution as well as the organization as a whole. To accomplish his purpose effectively, each must treat the other with the respect due his office. The company and the union have met on equal terms and adopted a contract recognizing each other's rights. Now each has its dignity to uphold. Organizations and corporations can act only through agents and representatives. To the extent that each treats the other with respect, the mutual job of resolving their joint problems will be enhanced.

Arbitrator Frank C. Pierson had a case which involved this point.

> While there is some uncertainty as to the exact words which were exchanged between Mr. G and Mrs. B, the arbitrator is persuaded by the testimony that Mr. G used improper language and that this language was directly related to Mrs. B's handling of certain grievances. The Company contends that Mr. G did not use expressions different from those customarily used in the plant and that Mrs. B was equally guilty on this score.... There are two points which have led the Arbitrator to reject these arguments of the Company. First, one of the Union's witnesses testified that Mr. G's language was "shocking" even in comparison to the "strong kind of talk" often heard in the plant. Second Mr. G used this abusive language in talking about official business with a representative of the union. The clear intent of the "no discrimination" clause which the parties included in the Agreement as quoted above, was to prohibit the employer from treating union representatives in an abusive manner just because they were carrying out their union responsibilities.
>
> It seems clear that Mr. G would not have talked to Mrs. B in the way he did if she had not been a shop steward, handling certain grievances for the Union. This fact, in conjunction with the particularly strong language he employed, convinces the Arbitrator that Mr. G discriminated against Mrs. B within the meaning of Article 1(B) of this Agreement.[12]

Clearly, where this type of management behavior and attitude is present, the union's representatives cannot function as equals with the company's representatives under the agreement. And where this occurs, the proper handling and resolving of grievances is inevitably frustrated by management's self-defeating behavior.

It is never wise for the foreman to conduct controversial grievance discussions with union representatives in the presence of employees not involved in the dispute. If for some reason the discussion becomes heated or out of control, the foreman can only lose in prestige, and the union representative will probably gain. Many union representatives enjoy and indeed seek an employee audience for their differences with management. A grievance discussion which has deteriorated to the point that it is out of control inevitably results in some erosion of the foreman's leadership with his work group. The adversary nature of labor relations is most conducive to this, and even reasonable men can disagree. Therefore, grievance discussions should be conducted privately, in an area and in an atmosphere where all principals can freely and fully explore the matter, thereby increasing the probability of arriving at an equitable resolution. The facts of the settlement can generally be made known to the interested employees subsequent to the grievance discussion. They need not witness its formulation.

As a management representative, an individual must assume a special responsibility for his conduct and behavior. He functions almost in a goldfish bowl, with the eyes of all hourly unit employees upon him gauging and weighing his actions and words. To preserve the status, authority, and integrity of his managerial position, he must be constantly aware of the impact his words and deeds have upon the employees and must conduct himself in a manner which enhances his position and does not detract from it.

As is true of many plants engaged in manufacturing operations, the use of colorful language is not foreign to the employees. Indeed, certain expressions are on occasion utilized by members of management as well. However, recognizing that colorful or profane words are sometimes commonplace in the industrial situation is not intended to endorse or encourage their use by a member of supervision. It is advisable for him or her to refrain from engaging in their use by exercising self-control.

To view these obligations differently would surely result in a derogation and act as a detriment to the legitimate interests of both the workers and management. It must also be recognized that the utilization of shop language by management personnel invites responses in kind from employees. In such an environment, the use of certain words or expressions by employees against supervision may be deemed as falling short of that quantum of resistance to industrial authority which provides sufficient cause for disciplinary action. Although an employee's or union representative's behavior may leave much to be desired, even perhaps slipping below the desirable standard of employee conduct vis-à-vis foremen, he may reasonably be considered to have had some justification because of the foreman's violation of the canons of proper supervisory behavior.

Physical Violence and Assaults

In the words of one court, "No looks or gestures, however insulting, nor words however opprobrious or offensive, can amount to a provocation sufficient to excuse or justify even a slight assault."[13] This is not precisely the extent to which arbitrators will go in judging cases where a union representative has assaulted a member of management, but there are some who may apply such a principle almost that literally. However, the majority will consider the case in light of the presence or absence of some type of provocation and weigh the nature of any provocation that may exist. As one arbitrator has commented, "If one is provoked or goaded by another's words or actions into acts of violence in the heat of anger, there may be grounds for some condonation of the offense."

An arbitrator ruled that the employer was entitled to discharge a union official who engaged in an altercation with his supervisor. The evidence supported management's claim the employee made a deliberate physical assault on his supervisor. The union's claim was that the attack on the foreman resulted from a remark attributed to the supervisor. Assuming the alleged remark had been made as claimed by the union, the arbitrator found it significant that about a half hour lapsed between the remark and the time of the attack. This lapse of time caused the arbitrator to remark: "If one has ample time to think over the remarks alleged to be provocatory and then acts violently, such violence must be looked upon as deliberate rather than provoked."[14]

Perhaps under these circumstances the union official would have been better off in the long run if his reaction to the alleged provocative remark had been instantaneous. It is obvious that his delay caused him to lose the right to claim that his assault had been provoked and not deliberate and premeditated.

Another arbitrator upheld a company's discharge of a union steward who attacked a supervisor and used profane language during the course of the scuffle. The grievant's behavior came after he had received a disciplinary notice for having left his work area, without permission, to write up a grievance protesting his supervisor's performance of bargaining-unit work. In this case the supervisor was not without blame. There was some evidence the supervisor might have grabbed the grievant in an effort to place a reprimand slip in his pocket. But even this could

not be considered sufficient provocation to excuse the attack that followed. The grievant admitted to attacking the supervisor on three occasions. By his own testimony, he was the aggressor. He admitted he
grabbed the supervisor by the shirt, then relaxed and let him go. By his
own admission, he used language for which there was no excuse. Also by
his own testimony, he grabbed his supervisor by the shirt for the second
time, and after the foreman pulled away, tearing his shirt in the move-
ment, the grievant attacked him a third time. Other witnesses stated the
supervisor was indeed angry, but it did not establish he was violent, so
the discharge was upheld.[15]

Where a member of management and an employee are equally at
fault, the outcome before an arbitrator will usually be much different
from the above case. Arbitrator John Day Larkin was involved in
deciding such a problem, where as a result of an altercation between two
such individuals, the employer discharged both parties. In his discussion
of the facts which precipitated the altercation, Arbitrator Larkin made
an interesting and telling observation:

> In view of the circumstances, the company might have been censored had
> it discharged [the hourly employee] and refused to discharge [the foreman].
> Out of all conflicting testimony in which each charges the other with
> primary responsibility for the "fight" incident, one cannot escape the feel-
> ing that *the two men should share the consequences of the unpleasantness for
> which they were jointly responsible.* There is unrefuted testimony that [the
> hourly employee] was something of a problem for his superior in the shop
> and that he used language which provoked [the foreman] to invite him out-
> side where the fight occurred. *[The foreman], on the other hand lost his
> temper and struck an employee – a thing which was indefensible.*[16]

There is an interesting aftermath to this story. Subsequent to the
discharge of both men, after being given a few days to cool off, both were
requested to return to the company for a conference with the president.
At these conferences, both men were told that they would be returned
to the payroll only if they resolved their differences and agreed to work
together peaceably. The supervisor agreed, but the hourly employee insisted that the foreman's discharge be confirmed and his rescinded.
Thereupon the president decided to reaffirm his actions of the previous
dates and maintain the discharge of both men.

Many are the published cases which have involved emotional or
angry management representatives who have either been solely at fault
or have been equally responsible for the difficult situations in which they
have found themselves. Another example of this is a dispute ruled on by
Arbitrator Charles G. Hampton where an employee was discharged for

an altercation with a supervisor. The effect of the supervisor's conduct on the final decision was readily apparent:

> The refusal of [the hourly employee] to ring out his time card when so directed would have been inexcusable if it had occurred without the previous "shoving" incident and the Arbitrator does believe, in the basis of the testimony, that [the foreman] shoved [the employee]. It is also apparent that [the employee] was intemperate in his language and attitude. In light of all the foregoing, this Arbitrator believes that both individuals were at fault and that, therefore, under the circumstances, a discharge was not merited but that some discipline was necessary. Therefore, the discharge shall be set aside.[17]

As a result of this sharing of guilt by the supervisor, the discharge could not be upheld. In another case with a similar conclusion, an employee was discharged for assaulting a foreman with a high-pressure water hose, the outburst of anger representing the culmination of several months of "riding" by the foreman. Holding that management had contributed to the employee's misconduct, Arbitrator A. J. Granoff descriptively recounted the reasons for his decision to reinstate the worker.

> Foreman T (an intelligent and promising young man), in his commendable anxiety to make good, involuntarily performed a disservice to himself and his employer. By throwing his weight around, all over his "kingdom" he at least broke the patience of a patient worker who had been silently taking his kind of "medicine" for weeks. T meant well but he did the right thing in the wrong way, falling into the costly habit of so many men who lose all humility on acquiring a little authority over their fellows. Thus he incurred the ill will of his men who fear and dislike him. He could have earned their good will and their confidence with much less effort, thereby maintaining, if not increasing, his men's efficiency. The time has long since passed when a supervisor can take undue advantage of his position to drive or abuse his men, or instill them with fear. Our industrial democracy protects the dignity and self respect of its workers. . . .
>
> T unquestionably goaded W into his outburst, the culmination of months of "riding." In our view of this case, this constitutes a substantial mitigating circumstance which must be taken into account, so that management must shoulder a portion of the blame for this employee's misconduct.
>
> So, with hesitation and considerable misgiving, we shall make an award which ordinarily should not be made in a case involving the serious overtones we have here. On the evidence as we see it, on our conclusions drawn therefrom, on the record as a whole, and on all the foregoing, the award

is that W be reinstated without loss of seniority, but with no back pay and with a strong reprimand which shall be taken into account in the event of any future breach of discipline on his part.[18]

The above case illustrates an extreme example of poor supervisory conduct. There a young, aggressive, and probably ambitious foreman who had not yet developed maturity of judgment in handling people was guilty of an excessive violation of discretion.

Off-Premises Problems

The locale for the discussion and exploration of grievance issues and plant problems is the place of work, not a tavern, a street corner, or anyplace else away from the work location. However, disputes and differences of opinion which originate in the workplace do sometimes get reargued and discussed off factory premises. Discussions and arguments of work disputes which occur off plant premises are always potentially more volatile. Employees and union representatives generally operate under the "misconception" that picking a fight with a supervisor is beyond disciplinary action if it occurs off plant property. This is not true. If the cause of the fight is connected to the employment relationship and the employee starts a fight afterward, he may properly be subject to disciplinary action.

It is all too evident that management personnel should not carry work problems to off-premises locations and engage in discussions or altercations relative to such problems. However, as mentioned earlier, the management representative may not be the one who becomes the aggressor. In fact, more often than not, he is the attacked rather than the attacker. When this occurs, there are certain things he can do. In a dispute between Goodyear Clearwater Mills and the Textile Workers, the employer imposed a four-day disciplinary suspension on an employee for inviting a supervisor "to come out to the gate and settle it" and laying his hand on the foreman's arm in a threatening and intimidating manner. In deciding the grievance contesting this suspension, Arbitrator Whitley P. McCoy offered these words of advice to the parties:

> When the Union requested Mr. O to reconsider his decision to lay W off for 4 days, Mr. O replied that he thought W had gotten off light. I am compelled to agree with that thought. If W had been discharged I would probably have felt constrained to sustain the discharge.
>
> No mill can stay in business if discipline is disrupted by such conduct. The mere invitation to the Gate, even without any laying on of hands, is conduct that cannot be condoned and still maintain order efficiency of operation.

It should be further noted, as a guide to future conduct, that there seems to be a misapprehension on the part of some employees that picking a fight with a supervisor is beyond disciplinary action if it occurs off company property. This is not true. If the cause of the fight is an occurrence on the job, and the employee starts a fight afterward, even though outside the Gate, he may properly be subject to disciplinary action.[19]

Another off-premises dispute occurred at a racetrack where a union official struck and abused a management employee after the latter had asked for a tip on the next race. Although the immediate cause of the attack had nothing to do with company business, the real cause of the attack was an incident which had occurred at the plant several days earlier when this management employee had reported this union official for being away from his work without a proper pass and thereby caused him to be reprimanded. Holding that the employer was justified in discharging the individual, the arbitrator concluded that the obvious purpose of the attack was to intimidate the management employee and thereby make certain that thereafter he would not dare to question the union official's movements in the plant. Had he succeeded in doing so unpenalized, it would have allowed him to continue to ignore the contract's requirements, and it would probably have had a harmful and demoralizing effect on the relations between the company and the employees in the plant.[20]

The next situation must have been a very difficult one for an arbitrator to decide. A union steward and a supervisor engaged in two fistfights outside working hours and off company property. The first was initiated by the union steward, who felt that the supervisor had applied company rules discriminatorily to him and had solicited employees to withdraw from the union. The second fight occurred an hour and a half later and was precipitated by the supervisor's unceremoniously kicking the grievant in the head when he found him apparently relieving air from his automobile tires.

Whether this second bout resulted from the foreman's belief that the union steward was meddling with his car, in which case it was not work-related, or grew out of the earlier work-related dispute was a hairy question for the arbitrator to resolve. Substaining the employer's discharge of the steward, the arbiter finally decided that the union had no contractual or other basis for questioning the company's relations with its supervisors or demanding that disciplinary action be meted out uniformly and in precisely the same manner between members of supervision and members represented by the union. This is not to suggest that he excused the behavior of the foreman – indeed he commented that it was highly improper–but the fact that the steward had threatened to "get" the supervisor and had precipitated the initial fight gave him no alternative. An interesting feature of the disputes was that the steward departed from these two confrontations with a cracked nose, a lump on his head behind his right ear, a bad cut in his mouth, and eyes almost closed, while the foreman experienced no physical damage.[21]

Among other off-duty activities arbitrators have held to affect the employment relationship, subject to company discipline, are the following:[22]

1. Where such conduct evinces a dangerous propensity, a criminal tendency, or serious emotional instability in the employee which is likely to manifest itself also on the job.[23]
2. Where a job feud is transferred outside the plant and there is a very real risk of a renewal of the feud on the job, or where the assault clearly arises out of the working relationship between the employees and not personal differences.[24]
3. Where off-duty behavior shows the employee to be a bad industrial risk.[25]
4. Where the behavior harms the company's reputation or product.[26]
5. Where the behavior impairs the efficiency or attendance of the worker, as through alcoholism.[27]
6. Where the conduct leads to refusal, reluctance, or inability of other employees to work with him.[28]

Chapter 6
Countermanding Management's Orders

For the most part, there appears to be unanimity of opinion among arbitrators about the impropriety of the union countermanding management's orders. Harry Shulman, a truly great spokesman and statesman in the arbitration process and former umpire with the Ford Motor Co. and UAW, articulated this wisdom:

> No committeeman or other union officer is entitled to instruct employees to disobey supervision's orders no matter how strongly he may believe that the orders are in violation of the agreement. If he believes that an improper order has been issued, his course is to take the matter up with supervision and to seek to effect an adjustment. Failing to effect an adjustment, he may file a grievance. But he may not tell the employee to disregard the order.[1]

In a similar dispute, although Arbitrator Feinberg reduced a discharge to suspension, he strongly censured a union-shop chairman:

> Certainly, a shop chairman has no right to countermand instructions given by management's representatives, whether or not he believes those instructions contrary to the terms of the collective bargaining agreement.... Any other arrangement would result in a chaotic condition in the plant and seriously interfere with production.[2]

The overwhelming weight of opinion in arbitral circles reflects the view that an industrial plant is not a debating society. When controversies arise, as they inevitably will, the operation of the enterprise must go on while the dispute is being discussed and resolved. The authority for directing that it go on is vested solely in supervision. The grievance procedure is designed to recompense employees adequately for abuse of authority by supervision. But the remedy under the labor agreement for violations of rights lies in the grievance and arbitration provisions and there only. For the union representative or the individual employee to disregard or countermand supervision's orders is to replace the grievance procedure with the extracontractual method of individual action. And such must be the advice of the union representative to his constituents. The only exceptions to this are orders which would require the employee to perform a criminal, unlawful, or immoral act. Also in this category are supervisors' directives which if carried out would jeopardize the health, safety, or welfare of the employees. But if the management order falls within such boundaries, the union representative's posture should be that the employee is obliged to obey the supervisor's instructions and seek redress and correction through the grievance procedures. The efficient and orderly operation of a plant requires that employees and union representatives alike respect the authority of their supervisors. And union representatives who advise employees to circumvent or disobey reasonable instructions issued by the company open themselves to disciplinary action.

Under an agreement which did not authorize compulsory overtime but did not prohibit it, management imposed two-day suspensions on members of the shop committee who requested employees to refuse to work overtime on a Saturday. These union instructions countermanded management's orders, and in interpreting the agreement the arbiter held that management retained the right to schedule the overtime. The discipline was upheld and the union's claim denied.[3]

The outcome of a case can be substantially influenced if there is a legitimate question whether management's instructions jeopardize the health, safety, or welfare of some employee. For example, a company was held not justified in discharging a union committeeman for usurping management's directional function by advising an employee he need not do an assigned job when both the employee and the committeeman sincerely believed the job to be unsafe. It was concluded that whether the job was actually unsafe or not, the committeeman could hardly have been expected to take the responsibility of advising the employee to take a risk when he honestly believed that job was dangerous.[4]

Where a union steward whose work record was characterized by substandard performance was discharged for reportedly countermanding his foreman's orders, the action was upheld by an arbitrator under a clause permitting discharge for "just and sufficient cause only."[5]

The line can be fine indeed between whether the union representative is countermanding management's orders or merely expressing an opinion to which he is entitled by virtue of his office. An example of this occurred in a case between the American Transformer Co. and the United Electrical, Radio and Machine Workers. The plant superintendent notified employees working on a job that there was no more work for them in this department. They were not to report to work on the following day, Thursday, but he would try to have half a day's work for them on Friday. When the chief steward was told about the instructions, he advised the plant superintendent that under the agreement the company was required to give the union 24 hours' notice before any layoff could be effected. In the absence of such notice, employees were entitled to compensation for half a day's work on the day following such notice. This entire discussion was held in the presence of the involved employees. At the arbitration hearing there was a considerable variance in the testimony. The chief steward and 10 employees testified that they had told the girls, "If you want to be paid for tomorrow, you report to work and I'll see to it that you will be paid." In contrast, the superintendent and a shop foreman testified that he "ordered" the girls to report for work the following morning.

The following day the company advised the chief steward he had been discharged for insubordination. His dismissal was based upon his order to the girls to report for work; such order issued was contrary to the orders of the plant superintendent. The arbitrator ruled that the chief steward should be reinstated with back pay on grounds that by explaining to the employees their rights under the contract, he fortuitously led them to disobey the order of their supervisor and it was his duty as a union official to explain the contract to the employees. Therefore, his conduct could not be considered insubordinate.[6]

If management is going to discharge a union official for ordering another employee to act contrary to the company's orders, it had better first give him an opportunity to explain himself and be certain its evidence will establish that the union official gave such a contrary order. This was a lesson learned by one employer in a dispute decided by Arbitrator Maxwell Copelof. The company discharged the union steward based on its claim he approached a toolmaker, a Mr. C who was at that moment operating a shaper in the tool room, and said, "I have to ask you not to run that shaper." Then it was alleged he told C that he had spoken to others, and as a result they were not operating the shaper. His reason for doing so was because it was "knocking shaper operators out of a job." The company claimed further that C informed his foreman of what the steward had said to him and asked for instructions as he had stopped his work on the shaper. Thereafter, the steward was advised of his discharge for this action. The union contended that in talking to his fellow worker, with whom he was on friendly terms, he was merely exercising his rights as a fellow worker in conformity with a practice prevailing throughout the plant – workers talking to each other while running their machines.

While the arbitrator was "fully aware of the apprehension enter-tained by the company concerning any attempt which might be made by union representatives to interfere with the company's rights to manage and direct its operations," he could not see that that had occurred here. He was not convinced that the steward was guilty of having attempted such interference. He did view the steward's talk with the other employee as "indiscreet," interpreted by C as an "order" to abstain from operating a machine. However, "the Company, in judging [the steward] on the basis of a report by C to the foreman, without having given [the steward] an opportunity to be heard and to explain his position, and con-demning him to the extent of summarily discharging him, was in the Ar-bitrator's opinion, extremely harsh, and could not be termed a discharge "for just and proper cause."[7]

The union's orders to employees to function in a manner contrary to a management directive need not take the form of a direct and clearly expressed instruction to the employees to operate in accord with its directions. Even though it takes the form of a milder instruction, if the employees respond affirmatively to the union's suggestions and in so do-ing react negatively to management's directions, the union officials responsible can be held to be functioning in violation of the labor agree-ment. This was the substance of an arbitral ruling under a collective bargaining agreement between the Joy Mfg. Co. and the International Association of Machinists.

The dispute grew out of an overtime assignment to two employees to perform a spray-painting operation on a product scheduled to be picked up later that evening by the customer's truck, which had come to the company's plant in Pennsylvania from Tennessee. When given the overtime assignment, both men agreed to work. Background informa-tion later proved that in protest of the handling of an overtime grievance, employees of the plant had been turning down overtime assignments for several weeks preceding this case. At the time of this grievance, the grievant in the prior overtime complaint was one of two spray painters assigned to the first shift. This grievant was the union committeeman who engaged the two scheduled overtime workers in some conversation in the plant's locker room just prior to his departure. Subsequent to that discussion with the committeeman, both employees changed their minds and informed management they could not work the overtime.

Management's investigation of the matter and the testimony at the arbitration hearing exposed the comments of the grievant to the two spray painters as a "reminder" that the plant employees were not work-ing overtime. There was no evidence that the reminder was coercive. Nor did it order the spray painters to refuse the overtime. Also, it did not threaten reprisal if they worked the overtime. However, the circumstances were not limited to what the grievant said to the two employees. As observed by the arbitrator, "Pertinent to the overall consideration is the fact that the grievant's comments were those of the steward of the paint department or those of a committeeman, as opposed to the comments of a fellow worker. As such, they would carry greater weight. Moreover, the 'reminder' was given not in a general and all-encompassing manner, but was rather directed to specific overtime to be worked that day by the two spray painters on this second shift."[8]

As mentioned earlier, one of the few exceptions to the rule that management's orders must be obeyed and protested later without employee or union right of refusal occurs when management's order jeopardizes the health, safety, or welfare of employees. An employer was held not justified in discharging a union committeeman for usurping management's function when he advised an employee that he did not need to do an assigned job because the employee and the committeeman genuinely considered the job unsafe and there was some evidence to support their views. A stubborn fact that could not be ignored here was that from the standpoint of these two individuals, there were reasonable grounds for their belief, and a union committeeman could hardly be expected to assume the responsibility of advising his employee to take a risk which he believed was involved. He was merely acting in the best interests of the employee and as a committeeman, which was his function. Based on those premises, the arbitrator reinstated the committeeman with full seniority rights and back pay from the time of his discharge.[9]

Chapter 7
Discipline and Discharge
of Union Representatives

Generally speaking, the most delicate type of discipline case is that which finds a union official the target of management's action. The dual role of the local union officer, as an employee and as an official of the labor organization, gives an added dimension to his conduct not shared by ordinary employees. In the role of employee, he has only the rights and privileges of other rank-and-file employees in his bargaining unit, and in this role he is governed by similar rules and regulations. While functioning in his job as an employee of the company, the requirements of attendance, punctuality, quality, production output, and the like are the same for him as for any other employee of the company. But while operating in his capacity of union representative, he enjoys a certain latitude and freedom in his day-to-day application, administration, and implementation of the contract. In this representational situation he becomes equal with the company's supervisors, thus enabling him to represent effectively and vigorously advocate the positions and interests of his constituents. Management's discipline or discharge of such a union official can frequently raise questions whether its action had antiunion or discriminatory motivation. Still another question may be was the union representative's act performed during a time when he was operating in his role as an employee, or was he acting as a union official?

Where the employee–union representative's misconduct has had only a tenuous connection to the fact he is a union official, it makes the arbitrator's job that much simpler. For example, an employer discharges an ice-cream driver-salesman after three instances of clashes with customers and fellow employees. The employee's entire five-year record was marked by instances of failure to carry out directions and assignments, uncooperativeness, sarcasm, and disrespect toward supervisors, belligerence and inability to get along with fellow employees, and discourteous conduct toward some customers. In sustaining management's action, the arbitrator found the union's charge that the employee was discharged for union activity without substance. There was no evidence of discrimination against the employee by the company, and only one of the many instances figuring in his discharge could have had any relationship to his duties as a union officer.[1]

On the other hand, an employee's behavior may involve actions of misconduct as an employee interspersed with abuses of his role as a union officer. Typical of this kind of case is one where the company discharged a union official who (1) threatened and intimidated employees regarding their joining the union, (2) carried on unauthorized union activity during working time, (3) engaged in and instigated horseplay while on the job, (4) took and retained another employee's wristwatch, and (5) failed to report for work as expressly directed by her supervisor.

Insubordination

In cases involving alleged insubordination by individuals who hold the office of union steward, if the steward was insubordinate as an employee, then penalties are generally considered proper. Such was the decision at the Dominion Electric Company where a union official refused a job assignment related to his tasks as an employee and the arbitrator concluded that the company did not discharge him with intent to discriminate but for his refusal as an individual to carry out a proper order.[2]

The principle must be affirmed that contract observance is the paramount responsibility of union officials since employees look to them for guidance in their contract obligations. Not the least of these obligations is the right to resolve differences through contract procedures. Union leaders as well as management representatives have to abide by these provisions, even at times of stress.

For example, a company discharged a chief steward who insisted upon immediate discussion of a grievance. Further, he refused to leave the plant to make scheduled deliveries until he talked with the plant manager and prevailed upon other union officers to call a meeting during working hours to discuss the grievance. Upholding the company's action, the arbitrator found that the steward's investigation of the union meeting was unnecessary under the circumstances and constituted a work stoppage in violation of the contract. The discharge penalty was supported by the steward's past record, which indicated that he had been misusing his union office and considered himself free to be on or off the job without concern for production needs, contract requirements, or supervisory authority.[3]

In a case with a different twist, the arbitrator sustained the discharge of a union steward who continually functioned in the capacity of a union official outside a fixed, agreed-upon hourly period established for stewards to handle grievances and otherwise discharge their duties. Although he was acting as a union official, his refusal to stop was in disregard of specific contractual regulations which limited the activity.[4]

But where the steward is "on union business," the usual requirement of "obey first, grieve later" is most often not applied by arbitrators if the orders given by management's representative are in conflict with the union's rights under the labor agreement. Such was the situation in a dispute decided by Arbitrator Whitley McCoy:

> There is a clear distinction between the case of a supervisor telling an employee to go back to his job and a supervisor telling the union to stop investigating a grievance. The company and union have met on equal terms and adopted a contract recognizing each other's rights. Each has its dignity to uphold. Organizations and corporations can act only through agents and representatives. When the duly authorized representative of the company told the duly authorized representative of the union to stop investigating a grievance, it was the company issuing orders to the union.... If he [steward] could rightly be penalized, it would put the entire grievance machinery, set up by agreement of the parties at the highest levels, at the mercy of supervisors with the possibility of great harm to the relations of the parties, even to a complete breakdown of the grievance machinery.[5]

Consider a case decided by Arbitrator Harry H. Platt where the sudden calling of a special membership meeting during working hours as a pressure device and with intent of causing interference with normal production was considered a "work stoppage" in violation of the contract. The arbitrator upheld the discharge of six union officials for aiding and causing it by carrying placards or passing out leaflets at the plant entrance. Contained in his comments on the propriety of this behavior is the following remark:

> The aggrieved were known union leaders, to be sure, but knowing of the influence they had to the other employees in the plant and being mindful of their responsibility as union representatives, to enforce compliance with the contract by its constituents, the company was right in tapping them as the leaders of the stoppage (a fact which, incidentally, the aggrieved have not denied) and very properly appealed to them to refrain from urging the other employees not to go to work.[6]

A case even more dramatic is found in a decision rendered by Arbitrator George E. Strong. Here also, members of the union's shop committee advised employees that the company would not have the right to invoke compulsory overtime and requested employees not to work on a Saturday. This action resulted in a loss of production for the air force and other customers. In supporting the company's disciplinary suspension of the union representatives, the arbiter considered the union's action, where a grievance procedure was available, close to abandoning the contract. Among the various astute comments he made in this connection was the following:

> A mass refusal of overtime work and the processing of a grievance are not simultaneous available remedies for any allegedly unauthorized requirement of compulsory overtime. The orderly procedure prescribed by the agreement was for the employees to work Saturday on protest and then file a grievance, or for the shop committee to file a union grievance. This was not done.[7]

Arbitrator Dudley Whiting rendered a different type of decision in a dispute where a union committeeman was discharged for refusing to perform assigned work which he believed was not covered by his classification. Arbitrator Whiting, concluding that the committeeman's trouble was due to overzealousness in his union office, reinstated him without back pay *upon the condition he resign from the office of union committeeman and pledge to remain out of such office.*[8]

Other Rule Violations

Insubordination is not the only offense for which union representatives may find themselves subject to discipline. While operating as an employee, all plant rules and other regulatory conditions which govern employee behavior are applicable to local union representatives. Union officials have found themselves in serious trouble with management for their transgressions in a number of areas. For example, the discharge of a union steward was found by Arbitrator Harold Gilden to be a warrented exercise of managerial discretion when the company established to his satisfaction that the steward was guilty of submitting false piecework tickets, thus claiming additional compensation for work which he was unable to prove he had performed in his bargaining-unit assignment.[9]

Then we have the situation where an employee–union president is discharged for excessive absenteeism. Where lies the proper balance between the latitude provided him in his capacity as union president and

his obligations as an employee? This was the question to be answered by
Arbitrator Harry Seligson in a hearing between Cessna Aircraft and the
International Association of Machinists. In examining this fact situation,
he made the following determination:

> To summarize: The Grievant was out an inordinate number of days for a
> variety of reasons: outside union business, illness, personal reasons. He
> was warned repeatedly about this, even to the extent of being given a
> disciplinary layoff. Although he was not occupying a key job in the depart-
> ment, it was a job necessary to the general operation of the department.
> Knowing that the company took a seriouis view of his absences and his leav-
> ing the job without first securing permission, he made little effort after the
> disciplinary layoff, to comply with the reasonable requirements expected
> of him, but continued to absent himself on Union business, aware on the
> basis of his previous record, that the chances were good that he might also
> be out for illness. Under these circumstances, I consider that the company
> has justified its charge of excessive absenteeism. The grievance is denied.[10]

Arbitrator David A. Wolff was faced with the problem of discharge
of a newly elected union officer for falsification of his employment application. While the officer was militant and aggressive and his discharge
followed by one day the union's strike vote over grievances he had been
processing, Mr. Wolff found that the employer's action was not
discriminatory or premised on his union activities. He commented:
"Whether or not he had been a union official his falsification would have
supported discharge. That he was a union official, would not mitigate
against the impropriety of what he had done.... The grievance is
dismissed."[11]

Arbitrator Charles G. Hampton encountered the problem of the
discharge of two union officials who drank on the job on Christmas Eve.
The arbitrator ruled drinking on the job was dangerous to the employee
and his fellow workers, and in this case it was also a direct violation of
the contract. Despite a union argument that both men were officers of
the local and that the company had failed to detect other employees
guilty of the same offense, he ruled that these considerations were immaterial and sustained the company's discharge.[12]

As stated earlier, sometimes the dispute may involve a question of
whether the employee was functioning as a union representative or an
employee. Such was the situation in a difference between the Goodyear
Decatur Mills and the United Textile Workers of America where a union
steward questioned the applicable piece-work rate for a job he was running. The management representative advised him he could not tell him
what the incentive standard would be until the job had been running long

enough for a computation to be made. The steward's position was that he wanted to know what the percentage was before he ran the job. When instructed again to return to the job, the steward persisted with his stand that he wanted to know the percentage before he ran it. When this was repeated still another time, he was ordered to leave the plant and was discharged. The union took the position that its representative was in the supervisor's office as a representative of the union, but according to the steward's testimony at the arbitration hearing, it was apparent that he was in the office chiefly because he wanted to know, as an employee, what his earnings would be.

The arbitrator considered it irrelevant whether he was operating in the capacity of an employee or a union steward:

> But if he was there as a union representative, his case stands no better. Officers and other representatives of the union, because of their position, owe a higher duty to the company in the matter of discipline than ordinary employees. B knew the terms of the contract . . . and had no right whatsoever to take the attitude he did. His continued insistence upon knowing the percentage, and his continued failure to return to his job, constitutes gross insubordination justifying discharge.[13]

It's not uncommon for arbitrators to weigh the length of time the union official has been in office and consider his degree of sophistication and familiarity with the scope of his union authority. Arbitral opinion often holds that a new steward's improprieties in office may be excused or partially justified by the fact that he is not completely informed. Such was the story in an International Harvester case when a union committeeman was disciplined for violating a company rule forbidding distribution of handbills on company property. The committeeman had acted in the honest belief that he was within his rights because of a recent NLRB decision involving a different company which found the company order prohibiting distribution of union leaflets on company parking lots illegal.[14]

Arbitrator Clarence Updegraff went a large step further in resolving a dispute over a discharged steward who on his first day in office told his foreman he was entitled to go where he pleased and proceeded to "roam" up and down in disregard of his foreman's repeated orders. Although he fully censured the behavior of this steward, Updegraff opined that:

> he would nevertheless have taken immediate proper directions from his own chief within the union, the divisional steward. However, this opportunity to give the inexperienced steward timely correction was ignored by the foreman. The green steward was given a further opportunity to repeat his mistake and to sink further into the consequences of his blunder. . . .

Modern personnel relations require from both sides and their representatives at least a reasonable degree of sympathetic tolerance. On the night
of the dispute, S was an inexperienced, newly appointed steward. *Management* appears to have been guilty almost of entrapment of the steward into
a harsh consequence of an ignorant mistake, instead of cooperation in a
charitable and tolerant effort to correct his erroneous assumptions [em-
phasis supplied].[15]

An issue often appearing in arbitration pertains to the discipline or
discharge of union representatives for actions which breach the contract.
Management's action may selectively impose different degrees of punishment. This most often occurs under agreements which contain provisions
allowing management discretionary decision making in its application of
a penalty. In other words, such agreements provide that the company
may either discipline or discharge participants in the illegal activity, with
the only issue allowed examination by the arbitrator being whether the
employees were participants. In such a case it is not incumbent upon
management to prove the extent of leadership on the part of discharged
employees since the arbitrator cannot be concerned with degrees of activity. If the contract provides latitude to the company in the remedy it
invokes, it limits the authority of the arbitrator. In cases of this type the
company may pick and choose. However, in almost all such cases the
union will claim that the company's decisions were discriminatory. Such
disputes are not easy ones for arbitrators to decide since they often leave
no choice but to disenfranchise employees from their jobs. From the company's point of view, discharge is often considered not too severe a penalty for a resort to economic pressure whereby untold hardships and inconvenience is suffered by many innocent and well-intentioned employees
and untold losses in dollars are suffered by the company as well as the
employees.

Typical of this kind of case was that between General American
Transportation and the United Steelworkers of America. The company
imposed three-day disciplinary suspensions upon 18 of 45 employees who
engaged in a strike in violation of the contract. Arbitrator Harry
Abrahams made an observation directly on the point:

The fact that twenty-seven (27) of the employees of the Company who did
not go to work were not given 3 day suspensions does not constitute
discrimination by the Company. The 27 employees involved were not on
the picket line and did not actively participate in keeping the employees out
on strike. In any event and in such a matter, the Company may select the
participating employees who will be suspended under the contract as was
done in this matter.

Under the contract involved, the company had the authority to discharge or otherwise discipline any employee who engaged in any strike, slowdown or stoppage of work. All of the employees who were given a 3 day suspension did engage in one form or other in the said illegal strike or slowdown, or stoppage of work.

The company in this matter was very lenient as it had authority to discharge employees who engaged in an illegal strike or work stoppage; but instead, the company gave the participating employees involved only a 3 day suspension.[16]

Sometimes management will allege that a "discharged" employee has quit, to shield it from the requirement of providing just-cause proof. The paramount initial question to be resolved in such a case is whether the termination of the employment was voluntary on the part of the employee or was brought about by some action or fault of the company. The consistent and uniform holding by arbitrators has been that an individual is deemed to have quit only when his conduct and words have demonstrated a clear and deliberate intent to quit. And although the company may attempt to call it a quit, more often than not it will find itself compelled to defend what really constituted a discharge action.

In a situation where a steward was called into the company's office and warned about advising foremen who were also union members not to perform bargaining-unit work, and employer representatives saw that the steward had clocked out 15 minutes later, the management official removed the steward's card from the rack on the presumption the steward had quit. Management took the position that he had rung out his card, walked off the premises, and quit. However, the steward returned shortly after clocking out, with another union representative. The steward maintained that he had merely rung out his card so he could go and telephone the union office for the representative to come and that he did not want to be accused of having wasted company time in making that call for the benefit of the union. The arbitrator held that the employee had in fact been discharged since the evidence indicated he had no intention of quitting and it further appeared that the company was looking for an opportunity to be rid of this steward. He considered management's action seizing upon the sudden ringing out of the card as a golden opportunity to achieve management's purpose without just-cause obligation.[17]

The outcome is different where there is controlling contract language which provides that employees may be construed to have quit their employment under certain conditions. This was the case under a contract with a no-strike clause which provided that employees who violated the clause "shall be deemed to have quit their employment." Governed by this circumstance, an employer was held to be justified in regarding as having quit two employees who over a period of time interfered with production by coming to the plant during their off hours and advising employees to limit their production. Additional misconduct consisted of blowing a plant whistle to signal employees to stop work and during the week prior to their termination spending nearly all their scheduled work time standing around idle while purporting to be on union business. A third employee was lumped into this same category when together with the other two, he threatened another employee with bodily harm unless he slowed down in his work.[18]

The basic principles of industrial discipline dictate that management must run its plant efficiently if it is to remain competitive. Intrinsic in the right to manage must be the right to administer discipline and maintain order. Equally important are the limitations on management's right to discipline under the just-cause concept found in most labor agreements. The processes of collective bargaining have substituted a system of law for the plant where the individual worker now receives many of the traditional safeguards of the shop court system with respect to his job.

Discharge is considered by many practitioners in the labor-relations field as the capital punishment of industrial life. The grievance procedure guarantees the worker the right to be confronted by his accused, to be represented, and to be ensured in the final decision that the punishment will be consistent with the offense. If it is found to be otherwise, the grievance and arbitration procedures guarantee his return to his job. The usual form of labor agreement imposes upon the company the burden of justifying its right to discharge an employee. In other words, if the company produced no evidence, an arbitrator would have no alternative but to reinstate the discharged employee with back pay. Therefore, in a discharge case, the burden of proof is generally on the company to prove that it had valid grounds for its action. In a typical case involving the discharge of a union representative, the union claims that management's action was discriminatorily motivated. When the union makes such an allegation, the burden of proof shifts to the union to prove its charge since the mere assertion that discrimination was the real motivation for the discharge does not establish it.

Arbitral Standards

Although parties to labor agreements have achieved and enjoy a higher level of sophistication than at any time in the past 25 years, cases involving discharge and discipline for union activities are still a frequent issue in arbitration. An analysis of the hundreds of published cases on these subjects may lead one to various conclusions. The parties have a long way to go before they achieve a desirable level of understanding of the rights and responsibilities of each. Perhaps it reflects in part the failure of both parties to assume their proper responsibility to train and instruct their representatives about the proper role of each. Perhaps it also reflects a failure of the parties to realize that each is here to stay, that each is entitled to its positions, principles, and philosophies, and that the only road to a peaceful and constructive relationship lies in mutual acceptance, respect, and understanding. But laying this aside and examining only the way most arbitrators view such disputes, arbitrators concur in their views regarding the bounds of union authority and the degree of behavioral freedom of the union representative. They impose the same criterion of just cause where discipline action is taken against the steward for alleged misconduct as an employee. When a claim is made of antiunion discrimination, in the absence of conclusive evidence of this, the burden of proof to support this claim falls on the union. But in judging such cases certain arbitral standards are used.

1. What has been the relationship between the parties? What is generally the atmosphere between the company organization and the union as an institution? And what has been the management representatives' relationship with the union representative being disciplined?

2. Is there any evidence of discrimination or union animus? Has the disciplined steward been a troublesome, aggressive militant individual—perhaps one who has filed many grievances or abused paid union time provisions of the agreement? If there is any evidence of union animus, the burden of disproving it in the instant case will fall on the employer.

3. Was there in fact a proven violation? Did the steward commit the offense of which he is accused? And can the company meet fully its burden of proof?

4. What has been the company's discipline treatment of other employees (nonunion representatives) for similar types of offenses where the circumstances were similar?

5. Was the union representative's conduct provoked? Did management's representative engage in similar conduct—threats, name calling, profanity, intimidation?

6. Did the incident, if provocative and inflammatory, occur in the presence of other employees, or did it happen in the privacy of a meeting between the principles only? And were the remarks and the behavior well beyond the customary shop vernacular and

mode of conduct customary in this context, that which is typical
and routine in this plant's day-to-day climate and atmosphere?

7. Was the union representative being disciplined new to his office,
recently elected or appointed, with little experience and understanding of his proper role and responsibilities? Was he a knowledgeable and informed individual with considerable experience
and understanding of his duties, rights, and obligations?

A management representative sensitive to the above criteria who
gives full consideration to each of these factors should find himself better
equipped to defend his action and have it sustained or supported by the
arbitrator. But the final answer to diminishing such problems rests in a
realization by each party of the rights of the other party. If the number
of such cases is ever to be reduced, each must assume its educational and
informational responsibilities and create an industrial atmosphere of
respect, understanding, and cooperation.

Chapter 8

Negative vs. Affirmative Leadership

It's generally recognized by arbitrators that local union officials not only have similar responsibility as other employees with regard to performance of their regular jobs but carry an additional burden of enforcing the contract and influencing other employees to comply with its terms. For example, where a union official participates in an unauthorized work stoppage, his offense is graver than that of the other employees.[1]

This concept was voiced by Arbitrator Arthur Hiller where the employer imposed a suspension against a shop steward for engaging in a strike in violation of the agreement.

> The proposition that affirmative obligations of leadership in upholding the grievance procedure and opposing work stoppages developed upon an employee, who by reason of seniority and status as a union officer must be held to have achieved a position of influence, has hitherto found acceptance under this and other agreements. Implicit is the thought that if those prominent and influential in the affairs of the union fail to so support these vital provisions of the agreement, the parties' expectations that they will be complied with during the life of the agreement become altogether illusory.[2]

Some arbitrators have even viewed a union official's passive behavior in the face of employee violations of the contract as a type of "negative leadership." One such opinion was expressed by Arbitrator Pearce Davis in a case where the local union president, union committeeman, and shop steward were disciplined for failing to attempt to prevent an unauthorized work stoppage.

> Local union officials are the spokesmen for the workers. They are their leaders. They, therefore, have responsibilities over and beyond those of the rank and file. Local union officials are obligated *aggressively* to *oppose*

actions that violate commitments undertaken in good faith. Local union officials are bound by virtue of their office to set personal examples of opposition to contract violation. They cannot be passive; they must vigorously seek to prevent contract violations by their constituents.[3]

Although it is clear that the majority of arbiters impart a greater responsibility to union officers for willful violations of the no-strike article, they will generally uphold a greater penalty only when violations are proved. For example, an arbitrator sustained the company's discharge of six union officials for aiding in and causing a work stoppage in violation of the contract by carrying placards or passing out leaflets at the plant entrance urging employees to attend a union meeting during working hours. The discharges were upheld despite the union's claim that other guilty employees went unpunished. In the first place, there was no proof that the company knew the identity of the other employees. And furthermore, since the other employees admittedly were not union officers, they did not have the same leadership responsibility as the discharged employees. However, he did not sustain the discharge of three other union officers where there was no proof that they had engaged in carrying placards or passing out leaflets.[4]

One arbitrator has indicated that a union agent's responsibilities under the agreement are comparable to those of management's representatives in upholding the integrity of the contract. In a Union Tank Car Company case with the United Steelworkers, the union claimed that a harsher penalty imposed against a union president than other employees participating in an outlaw strike was discriminatory. The arbiter said:

> While the effort may have been entirely unsuccessful, there was and is, nevertheless, a positive and affirmative duty on the part of the President of the Union, the Grievant, in good faith, to counsel and advise the membership not to engage in an unauthorized strike but to respect and follow the agreement and the grievance procedure....
>
> If, however, we should hold that union officers have no affirmative duty to see that the contract is respected on their side, then by what logic would anyone be justified in imposing any greater liability on the part of management to respect such labor agreement....
>
> We find that management had every right to expect the President of the Union, the Grievant in this case, to make every timely affirmative effort to prevent this outlaw strike, which clearly constitutes a violation of the agreement by the Union. It is not discriminatory to impose a penalty upon any employee who does not do all that he may reasonably be expected to do, in an effort to avoid a breach of the agreement by the Union members.[5]

The arbitrator upheld the discharge action, finding that the evidence was clear that the union representative participated and even instigated each incident, any one of which would have been considered just cause for discharge.[6]

In passing judgment on a union official's behavior, management must be particularly watchful not to apply a dual standard. To avoid a perception among employees that its motivation is one of union animus, it should give such individuals more than their share of reasonable doubt. Where management fails to do so, it is in danger of having its actions overturned by an impartial umpire. An employer was found not justified in discharging a shop steward for "creating a disturbance" when (1) the company made no effort to determine whether the steward had instigated the "disturbance" and (2) the employer permitted another employee, the obvious aggressor in the disturbance, to walk away with a "voluntary quit" on his record. The arbiter's ruling was that an employee caught up in an incident of violence, of neither his own making nor sustaining, could not reasonably be said to have engaged in "creating a disturbance."[7]

By virtue of his or her office, a union representative has a special obligation to observe and respect the agreement. It is his contractually recognized function to protect employees in the grievance procedure against violations of that agreement by management. The agreement gives him special rights and privileges in order that he may perform that function. He cannot with impunity turn his back on the very agreement which it is his duty to defend.

By virtue of his or her office, a union steward is a leader. It is reasonable to assume that it is because he is a leader that he acquires his union office. It follows that when a union steward participates in a work stoppage, making no effort to prevent it or bring it to a stop, he is setting an example for the other employees and indicating by his action that the stoppage has his approval and sanction. This is a graver offense than participation by an ordinary employee and justifies a more serious penalty.

One arbitrator upheld a two-week suspension of a union committeeman for aiding and encouraging employees to continue in a work stoppage in violation of the contract. Stopping short of requiring the shop committeeman to demonstrate affirmative leadership, he ruled as follows:

> The Arbitrator respects the attitude of the committeeman who is vigorous and militant in the assertion of the rights of the employees. At the same time, no committeeman is an island unto himself. He is part of a group of

people assigned by the Union to assist employees in bringing about a fair and proper administration of the collective agreement. This involves not only responsibilities to the men and the Union but also to the Company. There may be some argument as to whether there was an affirmative duty on the part of the grievant as committeeman when he came to the job site to tell the men to go back to work, but there can be no argument that he did not have the right, by his own conduct, to aid or encourage the men to continue in the work stoppage. The record is uncontradicted that the grievant did in fact by his conduct prolong a work stoppage which had begun prior to the time he had arrived at the job site. This was conduct which was not protected by such immunity as attaches to the role of Union committeeman.[8]

The preamble to an agreement stated that one of the purposes of the contract was to avoid strikes, slowdowns, and other disturbances which might interfere with production. The fact that this agreement did not contain the customary management clause did not operate to limit traditional management prerogatives. This is based on the well-established principle that a labor agreement acts to limit or restrict the usual management prerogatives which have not otherwise been limited or surrendered by some provision of the contract. The agreement also contained no specific reference to discipline or discharge of employees. But also assumed was that just cause was an implicit limitation upon the company's freedom to discharge.

The dispute arose around the company's discharge of the union's chief steward. Certain employees were on a form of incentive production, but the incentive rate for the paid task for a particular group had not been established. The company's contention was that the chief steward suggested or advocated a slowdown in the production. The company's action was based on evidence that three employees reported that the chief steward advised them to "slow down" production when the rate was off, pending resolution of a grievance as to the incentive rate. One of these three employees testified that the steward told them that as long as they were on the hourly rate, they might as well slow down since they wouldn't make more anyway. The end result of all this was that the employees did slow down in apparent response to the union steward's suggestion and contrary to the advice of their foreman. The arbitrator remarked:

> The grievant's testimony that she did not urge a slowdown but when the employees approached her concerning the rate grievance she told them they would be on the day rate until a new rate was established "and you work accordingly." On cross examination she said she told them while on

the day rate "work at the job steady, but don't kill yourself." On any interpretation of the evidence, the advice amounted to a suggestion not to work to capacity. The arbitrator is of the opinion that there is no basis for questioning the credibility of the company witness on this point. The conduct merited discipline of some sort.

It must be remembered that any conduct of the type involved represents an interference with the direction of the working force, a management prerogative. Whether this arbitrator would have imposed discharge instead of a lesser penalty, had the initial decision been his, is not relevant. Suffice it to say that discharge is in the range of reasonableness and, therefore, regrettably it must stand, despite the grievant's seniority.[9]

Another employer was justified in imposing a suspension upon a local union president who scheduled, sanctioned, and then refused to change the time of a union meeting which interfered with production. As a result of scheduling the union's meeting during working hours, over 600 of the plant's employees were absent from their work. It was customary in this factory for the local union to schedule meetings at two times to enable all employees to attend without missing work. Also, the employee–union representative's responsibility for calling special meetings in accordance with union bylaws did not obligate him to schedule such meetings at some specified hour or at a time which would cause some work interruptions. Finally, the employer took every possible action to attempt to head off this difficulty by appealing to the union president to change the meeting hour. Despite this, the president openly sanctioned the meeting, refused to change the time, and gave no indication that it was improper. By these actions he clearly lent support and encouragement to an illegal work stoppage. Also significant to the arbitrator was the fact that he was the first to leave the plant as a participant in the walkout.[10]

It is regrettable that it must be constantly repeated to some workers, and to some union officials, that if they are to continue to derive the full benefits of the victories the union has achieved for them in contract negotiations, it is mandatory that they conduct themselves responsibly and faithfully in delivering their commitments under the contract. Arbitrator Elmer Hilpert stated it even more flatly in a case involving the American Air Filter Co. and the Boilermakers local union where he found it necessary to uphold the dismissal of 132 participants in a work stoppage in breach of the contract: "Willing participation in a work stoppage is among the most heinous of industrial offenses; hence, the discharge of willing participants is not too severe a penalty (i.e., one which should shock the conscience of an arbitrator)."[11]

In a Ford Motor Company case with the United Auto Workers, Umpire Harry Platt upheld the discharge of a union president:

By his actions and no-action when he had a positive duty to act, he gave validity and leadership to the illegal strike and encouraged employees to continue it. He showed himself not a leader of men, as might be expected from one in the local presidency, but a captive of those who would destroy the agreement and the union's honor. He ignored his obligation to take affirmative action to halt the wildcat strike.[12]

Commenting on the injurious effect of such stoppages on the union, Arbitrator Harry Schulman, one of the truly great spokesmen for the arbitration profession, in an early case involving the Ford Motor Company and the United Auto Workers said:

> An illegitimate strike ... is not merely a breach of the contract. It is a serious blow against the union itself. It manifests a lack of confidence in the union. It mars the union's efforts to achieve compliance by the company. It weakens the union's bargaining power in future negotiations. It is a blow to the union and its membership as it is to the company. All three must be equally concerned with its control.[13]

Too often, union officials or employees who have been unsuccessful in achieving their aims at the bargaining table or in prior discussions involving grievances resort to self-help. While they aggressively maintain the right to enjoy all of the benefits secured under the agreement, they consider it advantageous to ignore their responsibilities under this contractual instrument when they are dissatisfied with the obligatory provisions which apply to them. Of course, such conduct cannot be condoned. If allowed to conduct themselves in this fashion, there would be no need for an agreement between the parties. With this type of jungle atmosphere, each party could accept that part of the agreement beneficial to it, rejecting the balance. The chaotic result would be a dangerous instability in the labor-management relationship and would destroy the very purpose for which the parties have constructed the agreement.

Continuing our examination of the arbitral view on the concept of negative versus affirmative leadership, Arbitrator Saul Wallen stated it as follows:

> The union leadership has an especial responsibility to honor the pledged word of the union to abide by the agreement's restraints in exchange for garnering its benefits. The leaders of any organization, in return for the satisfactions of leadership–the sense of power, the rewards of personal satisfaction and the prerequisites of the office–must accept the responsibilities as well. At the very least, these include the obligation to refrain from promoting, encouraging or condoning an illegal walkout.[14]

Arbitrator Vernon Stouffer, in a dispute between Phillips Industries and the Sheet Metal Workers Union, upheld the dismissal of 19 employees, including some union officials, who participated in an unauthorized strike. He noted that although the officers had made some ineffectual attempts to get the employees back to work, the officers did not return to work, even after an injunction was issued and pickets removed.[15]

If there is one principle universally recognized in the field of industrial relations, it is that union representatives have the highest duty to adhere to all of the provisions of the collective bargaining agreement and to instruct other employees to do so. Under a contractual no-strike article, where it is improper for an ordinary employee to breach the contract, a similar act by a union representative is totally untenable. There can be no argument that the stability and orderliness of a collective bargaining agreement, as well as its sanctity, depend upon adherence to its provision that there shall be no strikes or lockouts during its term. It is a well-established principle that union representatives share an obligation to set an example for all employees within their jurisdiction by demonstrating a loyalty to the terms and conditions of the contract. Only in this way can the union representatives comply with their responsibility to uphold the integrity of the contract and its orderly grievance and arbitration processes for the settlement of disputes.

This universally recognized principle is not mere academic philosophy to the parties under a labor agreement. Even high-ranking international union officials concur with this concept. The situation grew so bad between the United Parcel Service and the Teamsters that it led the international president James Hoffa to reiterate this principle in a letter to "all officers and stewards" of this local. The pertinent parts of his letter were quoted in a published arbitration decision resulting from one such work stoppage at this location. Hoffa expressed this principle as follows:

> It has come to my attention that some of your stewards and members employed at United Parcel Service, Inc. have again engaged in an unlawful and unauthorized work-stoppage in violation of your collective bargaining agreement. This is the second time this year that such a major, unauthorized stoppage has occurred. These unauthorized stoppages are not only in violation of the contract, but they also represent an exercise of authority by stewards which is beyond their power under the contract and which subjects them to removal from office under Article 9, Section 2 of your Local Union Bylaws.
>
> In view of the history of unauthorized stoppages at United Parcel Services, Inc., in violation of contractual commitments and in violation of

Local Union Bylaws and the International Constitution, I feel it is my duty to warn all officers and stewards that a continuation of this type of unjustifiable activity cannot be tolerated by the International Union, and should not be tolerated by the Local Union.

Additionally, of course, the members and stewards who are involved in these unauthorized contractual violations must be aware that neither the local union nor the International Union are in any position to protect their jobs, their job rights or their seniority when they engage in these unlawful activities.

It is my request that the Local Union Executive Board immediately cause duplicate copies of this letter to be prepared and distributed to every steward at United Parcel Services, Inc., and also posted on all union bulletin boards so that the stewards and the membership may be informed of the seriousness of the situation and the possible consequences of any further unauthorized work-stoppages in the future.[16]

The collective bargaining agreement is just as binding on the union and the employees as it is on the company. Such contracts contain grievance procedures and arbitration arrangements for the resolution of any controversy which arises out of a breach by the company. The proper method in settling such disputes is through these contractual procedures. Both statutory and decisional law in this country require the settlement of industrial disputes through the use of such peaceful procedures and condemn the use of outlaw activities in violation of such contracts where they contain provisions for grievance and arbitration. It is in anticipation that the parties will experience differences between them and that contract violations of one sort or another will occur during the term of the contract that they have agreed upon these more peaceful arrangements.[17]

Where such union obligations were disregarded by the union's officials, an arbitrator upheld a three-day disciplinary suspension of three shop committeemen who participated in a slowdown and gave the slowdown tacit if not active sanction.[18] This was the ruling, although not all employees engaging in the slowdown were disciplined. The employer was unable to identify ringleaders and chose the next most effective device by making examples of those guilty employees who had undertaken the responsibility of providing leadership for shop employees.

But if there are two sides to every issue, there is another arbitral viewpoint to the question of the greater responsibility of union representatives. To attempt to give space if not credit to this contrary point of view, a review of such cases may be in order. Nowhere was this more apparent than in a case where an employer was deemed not justified in discharging a union committeeman who participated in a wildcat strike, on the premise that the committeeman neither incited nor led the strike and no other employee who participated in the strike was penalized. This arbitrator opined that the fact that the discharged employees were union officers did not warrant a greater penalty than those imposed upon other employees. The responsibility and higher duty owed by committeemen as union officers was not to the company but to other employees and the union.[19]

Chapter 9

Representation of Employees in Meetings and Interviews

The principal objective of the grievance provisions of a labor agreement is to afford assistance and advice to the employee who is involved in a disagreement with management. The typical labor agreement manifests the mutual desire of the parties to have grievances satisfactorily resolved without undue delay. Most contracts set forth procedures contemplating that the union representative will exercise his responsibility and authority to discourage grievances where the management action appears to be justified. The grievance machinery is the creature and the servant of the parties and has been purposely adopted by them to resolve disputes arising under the agreement. The presence of the union representative in the grievance procedure must be regarded as a factor conducive to the avoidance of formal grievances through the medium of discussion and persuasion conducted at the threshold of any impending grievance. It is not unreasonable to expect nor illogical to assume that the union representative will utilize his office in appropriate cases to limit formal grievances to those which involve differences of substantial merit. Of course, the extent to which this objective is accomplished is materially dependent upon the faith of the parties and their willingness to be amenable to reason and persuasion.

Under the agreement, management's representatives are bound to decide and act in a manner consistent with the letter and spirit of the agreement. Failures on the part of these company agents may be subject to challenge through the grievance procedure. Union officials under the contract are required to represent all employees in the bargaining unit for the purpose of collective bargaining of wages, hours, and other terms and conditions of employment. And this obligation is stretched by the law to embrace a representational obligation of employees, whether members of the union or not. Although courts have held that unions are accorded broad discretions in their handling of individual grievances, they owe a duty of fair representation. Violations of this pledge can bring them liable to damages for breaching their duty.

The scope of a union representative's duties, rights, and obligations to represent employees is governed by the terms of the collective bargaining agreement and the Labor Management Relations Act. Section 7 of the act entrusts employees with the right to bargain collectively through their chosen representatives. Sections 8(a)(1) and 9(a)(5) provide that an employer's refusal to respect this right constitutes an unfair labor practice. *Collective bargaining* is defined by Section 8(d) of the Act as "the performance of the mutual obligation of the employer and the representative of the employees to meet at reasonable times and confer in good faith with respect to wages, hours and other terms and conditions of employment."

In interpreting and administering this law, the National Labor Relations Board has recognized that an employee's right to union representation does not apply to all dealings with his employer which may eventually or ultimately affect the terms and conditions of his employment. For example, in a Chevron Oil Company case the board held that the exclusion of union representation from an employer-employee interview was not unlawful. There, a foreman had reported that nine employees had walked off the job 15 minutes early in defiance of his orders. The employer interviewed the employees prior to arriving at a decision on disciplinary action. The board concluded that such a fact-finding meeting was merely an added effort on the company's part to hear both sides of the situation before reaching a decision, and it pointed out that employees should not be shielded by a bargaining agent from company inquiries when management embarks upon an investigation to ascertain whether plant discipline has been breached.[1] Similarly, in a Jacob-Pearson Ford case, the board upheld the employer's denial of a requested union presentation at a proposed meeting between the company and its procrastinating employee, ruling that such meeting was called merely to gather information. In other words, the board and many courts have generally held that where employer interviews of employees deal only with eliciting facts and not with the consequence of the facts which are revealed, its subject matter is not within purview of compulsory collective bargaining.[2]

In a refusal-to-bargain charge brought by a union against the employer, the board held that the company did not violate the LMRA when it refused an employee union representation at a meeting dealing with the employee's refusal to accept a job assignment. This was notwithstanding the union contention that the employee faced "potential" discipline where the potential discipline was remote and the purpose of the meeting was essentially for gathering information. When the employee was invited to meet alone with the company, management had not reached its decision to discipline him but was investigating facts concerning the refusal of a job assignment. Furthermore, the employer promised to furnish the union with an explanation of any decision reached as a result of the meeting and to pursue the meeting further at the bargaining table.[3]

In a case before the board in which the author was personally involved, an employee after six months suspension was reinstated by his local union as its chief steward, and the union formally notified the employer of his reappointment. Ten days after receiving this communication from the union, the company wrote to the president of the local union stating that this appointment "does not accord with the provisions of the agreement between the parties." The employer also orally informed the union president that it refused to deal with this individual as chief shop steward because he was no longer an employee of the company and suggested that someone else be appointed in his place. (As a point of information, the reappointed chief steward had been discharged by the employer prior to this latest reappointment but subsequent to his initial suspension by the union from office.) After so advising the union, the company refused to meet with this individual as chief shop steward when he attempted to process employee girevances against the company. In deciding this dispute, the board examined the contractual language and wording of the grievance procedure, precontract negotiations, and testimony as to established practices under the agreement.

Under the act, a union, as the duly designated representative of the employees in the bargaining unit, has the right to select persons, whether employees or nonemployees, to negotiate with the employer on grievances. Therefore, the company may not, without violating the act, insist that the union surrender this right as a condition of entering into a collective bargaining agreement. But while a union may not be compelled to give up its right to be represented by any persons it wishes, it may waive this right voluntarily during collective bargaining.

During the negotiations leading to this agreement, the question of the union's representation in the grievance procedure was explored by the parties. Revisions were agreed upon which prohibited participation in the grievance procedure by any union representative who was not employed by the company. By so agreeing, the union voluntarily waived its right to be represented in the grievance procedure by representatives who were not members of the bargaining unit and employees of the company. So finding, the board ruled that the employer's refusal to discuss employee grievances with this individual was not a violation of the act.[4]

The absence of union representatives from employer meetings with employees did not constitute a refusal to bargain under the act where the purpose of the meeting was merely to disseminate information concerning a profit-sharing plan. It had previously been negotiated by the parties during collective bargaining leading to a new labor agreement. The provisions of the profit-sharing plan had been established at that time and incorporated in the agreement. The employer held the meetings as part of a basic routine to inform newly eligible employees of their coverage and benefits. No negotiations took place, nor did the company bargain directly and individually with the employees with respect to rates of pay, wages, or other conditions of employment. Neither did it attempt unilaterally to change the plan. Also brought out by the board was that it was neither customarily nor generally the practice for union representatives to be present at meetings of the employer and individual employees concerning their insurance benefits, Blue Cross Accident and Sickness insurance, and personal problems.[5]

The duties owed by unions to employees in handling grievances are fully examined by Hauslowe in "Individual Rights in Collective Relations," 45 Cornell L.Q. 25, 46:

> It is arguable that, whatever the needs for flexibility and wide discretion in the negotiation of new or modification of existing collective contracts, no such flexibility is either needed or appropriate when rights under a contract are involved. The standards for judgment in this area have been less than perfectly formulated. In general terms they are frequently stated as follows: The Union's conduct must not be willful, arbitrary, capricious or discriminatory. The Union must not have declined to press the grievance out of laziness or prejudice, or out of unwillingness to expend money on behalf of non-members. Its decisions with respect to individual grievances must have been honest and reasonable.
>
> The rejection of a grievance by the Union must have been on the merits, in the exercise of honest discretion and-or sound judgment, following a complete and fair investigation. The rejection must not have been unjust in any respect. There must not have been bad faith or fraud. The bargaining agent must not have acted in a negligent manner.

In handling the grievances of nonunion members, the parties should be aware of two provisions of the act with regard to the rights of employees. In Section 7 of the act:

> Employees shall have the right to self-organization, to form, join or assist labor organizations, to bargain collectively through representatives of their own choosing, and to engage in other concerted activities for the purpose of collective bargaining or other mutual aid or protection, *and shall*

also have the right to refrain from any or all of such activities except to the extent that such right may be affected by an agreement requiring member- ship in a labor organization as a condition of employment as authorized in Section 8(a)(3).

The second provision of the act which most often comes into play under this type of union-security clause is Section 9(a):

Representatives designated or selected for the purposes of collective bargaining by the majority of the employees in a unit appropriate for such purposes, shall be the exclusive representatives for all employees in such unit for the purposes of collective bargaining in respect to rates of pay, wages, hours of employment, or other conditions of employment: provided, *that any individual employee or a group of employees shall have the right at any time to present grievances to their employer and to have such grievances adjusted, without the intervention of the bargaining represen- tative, as long as the adjustment is not inconsistent with the terms of a col- lective bargaining contract* or agreement then in effect: provided further, that the bargaining representative has been given opportunity to be pres- ent at such adjustment.

The grievance process must be afforded to nonmembers as well as union members, and on the same terms and conditions. Any grievance should be viewed in the light of the basic standards established by the terms of the contract between the company and the union. All grievances, including those from nonmembers, must be limited to prob- lems within the scope of this standard. Any relief or remedy applied must not violate or undermine this basic standard.

Under the "Management Right" clause, the company has retained the right to manage and direct the working forces. In so doing, its repre- sentatives must necessarily converse and discuss with employees, issue them instructions and orders, ask them questions, give them informa- tion. It may not "bargain" with them individually regarding their wages, hours, working conditions, and so on. It may not endeavor to enter into individual "agreements" with them covering such subjects.

The subject of individual rights in collective bargaining has been ex- tensively discussed for several years now. Problems arise because our concept of individual rights arose in a simpler society where it was enough to protect the individual against the power of the majority in- stitution. The principal technique used was to limit the power, for exam- ple, of the state, as in the Bill of Rights. However, the desirability or perhaps inevitability of powerful institutions has now been established, and the problem is to protect the individual within the powerful institu- tion, but without weakening the functioning of that institution.

It has been held that the above-quoted proviso, Section 9(a), grants to individual employees the right to process their own grievances. The New Jersey Supreme Court even went so far as to hold that as a matter of federal law, an individual employee had vested right under this section of the statute not only to present his grievance to his employer but to take his unsettled grievance to arbitration, notwithstanding the refusal of his union to do so. A different ruling issued from the Court of Appeals of the Second Circuit in the case of Black-Clawson Company and the International Association of Machinists. This court presented the view that Section 9(a) merely gave the company the freedom to consider grievances presented by individual employees; further, that this proviso would not grant an employee a substantive right requiring the company to take up his grievance. The court ruled that an employee as an individual had no standing to compel arbitration since the terms of the collective bargaining agreement provided access to arbitration only to the union and the employer. This court stated that Section 9(a) did not confer upon individual employees the power to compel an employer to entertain the grievance or channel it through the arbitration process. The relevant part of this decision stated:

> Our conclusion is dictated not merely by the terms of the collective bargaining agreement and by the language, structure, and history of Section 9(a), but also by what we consider to be a sound view of labor management relations. The union represents the employees for the purposes of negotiation and enforcing the terms of the collective bargaining agreement. This is the modern means of bringing about industrial peace and channeling the resolution of intra-plant disputes. Chaos would result if every disenchanted employee, every disturbed employee and every employee who harbored a dislike for his employer, could harass both the union and the employer by processing grievances through the various steps of the grievance procedure and ultimately by bringing an action to compel arbitration in the view of clear contractual provisions intended to channel the enforcement remedy through the union.

This case was cited with approval by the Supreme Court in *Republic Steel Corporation v. Maddox*. The Court declared that individual employees could not bypass their bargaining agent and the contractual grievance procedure to claim their rights under a labor agreement in a lawsuit. Therefore, under the current state of federal law, individual employees do not have a right to arbitrate claims under a union agreement. A company can rest fairly assured that entering an agreement to arbitrate claims which arise under the contract with the union will probably not lead to individual employee harassment through lawsuit or private arbitration. Of course, the extent to which this is true will be influenced by the particular wording of the labor agreement and whether it provides access to individual employees.

The foregoing has been a brief examination of court and board rationales to provide a flavor of how such forums have viewed a union's duties, rights, and obligations of employee representation. Volumes could be written on the legal coverage which has been afforded such material, including the provocative issue of individual rights. No attempt has been made here to treat this subject fully, only to provide a taste of the medicine administered by the courts and the NLRB to allow a fundamental insight into the breadth and complexity of such questions.

Just as important to the practitioner in the area of labor relations is the reasoning employed by arbitrators. Some such issues are presented in that arena, and it is to an examination of a few such cases that we now turn. Putting the cart before the horse, a case will first be explored where the issue dealt with the management's right to bring a representative of its choosing into a third-step grievance meeting. During the term of a labor agreement the vice president of the company had a company attorney accompany him in third-step grievance meetings to assist in handling grievances initiated by the union. This provoked the international representative of the union to refuse to meet with the vice president as long as the company counsel was present. Relying upon a strict construction of the contract, the union representative stated that he would meet with the vice president or with the labor counsel as a designee of the company, but not with both. The company persisted in continuing to have labor counsel present whenever a third-step grievance meeting was scheduled, and several such meetings were adjourned without progress when the union refused to meet with both company representatives present. Finally the union grieved, the company claiming it had a right to have its legal counsel present, and the union appealed the matter to arbitration. Faced with controlling contract wording which made it clear that the vice president of manufacturing alone represented the company in discussing and handling grievances at the third step unless he decided not to do so, in which event he had to elect a designee, it seemed obvious to the arbiter that only the vice president or his designee (not both) was to handle, discuss, and argue such grievances. The language did not preclude the vice president or his designee from having company counsel or other individuals present to advise him. However, such individuals were precluded from participating or entering into discussions concerning the grievance. Their participation had to be limited to giving advice to the vice president or a designee.[6]

It is customarily recognized that it would be difficult if not impossible for management to direct its working force effectively if every employee was entitled to have a union representative present whenever a foreman spoke to him. Certainly this is not the requirement of law or the typical contract when management is engaged in its regular business of directing its work force. But at what stage in a typical procedure is an aggrieved employee entitled first to demand representation in the handling of his grievance? Under a labor agreement which indicated that a grievance existed when an employee "believes that he has been unjustly dealt with" or that the contract has been improperly applied, where the matter had been discussed by a shop steward with the foreman, an employer was found not justified for discharging for insubordination an employee who refused to discuss an incipient overtime grievance with management in the absence of the union representative. Based on the contract language as well as pertinent decisions of the NLRB, the employee was within his rights in insisting upon the presence of a union representative during the discussion of a grievance which was clearly in its formative stages. The rationale for excusing the insubordination was that the employee was not required to obey the company's demand to file a grievance because the order the employee refused to obey was not a work order but one which interfered with his right to full use of the grievance procedure.[7]

Employers should be careful to comply in good faith with provisions of the agreement dealing with employees' rights to union representation and any unreasonable denial thereto. Rejecting an employee's legitimate demand for union representation at a time when management is imposing a disciplinary action can result in a negation of that management action by some arbitrators. A perfect example of this occurred under a contract which stated that employees appearing before the company for the purpose of adjusting grievances or disputes, including discharge, "will be given the right to have the plant steward or committee present if he or they so desire." A discharged employee whose request for the committee's presence at a meeting preceding his discharge was denied by an employer was reinstated without back pay, even though the discharge was for good cause. Because the grievant was not permitted to have the committee present, his discharge was not, in the opinion of the arbitrator, for good cause. However, because other behavior as an employee was deserving of his penalty, he was reinstated without back pay. Had the company accorded with the contractual requirement to have the committee present, a reading of this case suggests that the discharge would have been sustained.[8]

Chapter 10
Areas of Stewardship

Union representatives have areas of authority, areas of responsibility, and areas within which they may exercise and utilize their stewardship. It is not uncommon for parties to enter labor agreements in which they have specifically identified by title the union representative who will function under the agreement and further to define or delineate the geographical area of operation of the union official. Such contract language may either limit a union official to function in a given step of the grievance procedure or may outline the geographical boundaries and factory limitations within which the union official may operate, or both.

In 1984, the U.S. Department of Labor issued its Bulletin 1425-2, a study of grievance procedures. Virtually all (99%) of the labor agreements studies included a procedure for handling grievances. The study was based on an analysis of 1,717 collective bargaining agreements, each covering 1,000 workers or more, representing almost all agreements of this size in the United States, exclusive of railroad, airline, and government agreements.

A particularized study of 416 of these agreements regarding the "initial presentation" stage of the grievance procedure indicated that the parties permitted to submit a claim to the grievance procedure were identified in 395 of these agreements. All of those agreements which did not indicate who presented grievances initially were multiemployer agreements. These 416 contracts covered the work situations of over 2.6 million workers.

It is interesting to discover that almost two-thirds have definitely identified the initiating parties involving both the employee and the union representative. Practically all of the contract provisions among this two-thirds majority allowed the steward (at the employee's option) to accompany an employee, permitted either the aggrieved employee or the union representative or both to present the grievance or allowed the employee to accompany the steward on presentation of the complaint.

	Agreements	Workers
	416	2,600,000
Initial presentation by		
Employee and/or union steward	238*	1,625,700*
Union	71	516,000
Steward	37	94,300
Employee	20	67,400
Business agent	15	132,900
Grievance committee	11	55,800
Business agent and/or steward	3	8,300
Not clear, or varies by local agreement	3	4,800
Not indicated	18	95,100

*Because of rounding, figures may not equal totals.

For example, a provision from an agreement between Otis Elevator and the IUE: "The grievance shall first be presented by the aggrieved employee in person, and, if he so desires in the presence of his *department steward to the shift* or immediate foreman to whom the employee is working. The department steward shall be given an opportunity to be present at the adjustment of the grievance." It is suggested by the language that the only appropriate union official to represent an employee upon initiation of a grievance would be the steward who was in his department and was on his shift.

The review of a different contract, this one projecting a different inference, is one between Acme-Newport Steel and the United Steelworkers. This contract provided in part: "Any such employee may . . . report the matter directly to his grievance or assistant grievance committeeman and in such event the grievance or assistant girevance committeeman, if he believes the request or complaint merits discussion, shall take it up with the employee's foreman in a sincere effort to resolve the problem. The employee involved may be present in such discussions, if he so desires." Standing alone, this provision does not clearly stipulate which of the two union representatives must participate, either the grievance committeeman or the assistant committeeman being eligible, and the language does not specify their whereabouts with regard to any geographical locations.

Some agreements outlined qualifications employees had to meet in order to be eligible to hold union office. Where any such qualifications were specified, they were most uniquely phrased to require that shop stewards or other union representatives be employees of the company. It was also not uncommon for a minimum length of service to be required of those employees aspiring to union office. An example of this is contained in the language of a contract involving Commonwealth Edison and the IBEW. "Only regular employees of the company, employed in the respective work groups they represent, shall be designed as steward, chief steward or members of the joint union board."

Another sample comes from a collective bargaining agreement between International Harvester and the UAW:

> No person shall be eligible to serve as steward or grievance committeeman or their alternate except an employee in the bargaining unit who has acquired seniority status, provided however, that in the event a new department is created within a bargaining unit covered hereby and a majority of employees in such department are probationary employees, this provision will be waived for said department.

This Department of Labor study further showed that unions generally wanted to bring in higher-level representatives who were not employees of the company to deal with higher levels of management in the grievance procedure. Such outside representatives were usually full-time union employees or officials – a business agent, the local union president, regional or international union representatives, and in a few cases officers of the international. Typical of such clauses was that between General Telephone Company of Pennsylvania and the IBEW: "It is understood that an international representative of the union may be present on the union's behalf during step 4 and onward."

Another example comes from the Monsanto Chemical Corporation – Plastics Division and the IUE: "The business agent of the union, or other authorized union representative, will be recognized to assist in the settlement of grievances which have been referred to step 3."

Although it was seldom encountered, a few agreements provided that *outside* union representatives could handle grievances at all steps. A few other agreements permitted outside union representatives access only after the earlier steps of the grievance procedure had been exhausted.

Leaving this study and turning to an examination of contract clauses which have appeared in major collective bargaining agreements across the country which relate with greater specificity to "areas of stewardship," the following comes from an agreement negotiated by the United Automobile, Aircraft and Agricultural Implement Workers:

102(U). The Union will be represented by the following representatives for the exercise of the functions specified in this article and who, in order to qualify and be recognized by the Company as such, shall have been employed by the Company continuously for at least 6 months.

(a) A plant committee of not more than five members; the functions of this committee shall be to serve:

1. as a collective bargaining committee, and

2. with respect to grievances under steps (c) and (d) of section 1 of Article III hereof; and under section 1 (b) of Article IV hereof.

(b) Three Chief Stewards, one for each shift, functioning plant wide whose function will be limited to handling grievances under steps (b) and (c) of section 1 of Article III hereof.

(c) One divisional steward on each shift for each division; the function of these stewards will be limited to handling grievances in accordance with steps (a) and (b) of this section.

(d) Alternate stewards on each shift in each division who shall function only during such time as the regular stewards may be absent form the plant Alternate chief stewards may function only during such times as the regular chief stewards may be absent from the plant or engaged for a protracted period of time in collective bargaining as a member of the Bargaining Committee.

The divisions referred to herein are listed below, it being understood, however, that in the event new divisions are added, reduced, or changed, the number of stewards may be changed accordingly.

This provision requires the union representative to meet certain criteria with regard to holding union office as well as areas within which he functions. He must first have a minimum of six months' service with the company; chief stewards may operate plant-wide on their shift; divisional stewards may function on their shift and their division and operate only within certain steps of the grievance procedure. The clause specifies the numbers of union representatives who may serve at any one time.

For comparison, let us look at another collective bargaining agreement by another employer whose employees were represented by the same union:

105(U). Employees shall have the right to be represented by a Bargaining Committee if six (6) members, all of whom shall be regular employees of the Company.

For the purpose of representation of the employees by the Bargaining Committee, the Plant will be divided into six (6) zones.

One member of the Bargaining Committee will be assigned by the Union to each of these Zones, for the purpose of investigating and negotiating with respect to Grievances as outlined in the Grievance Procedure hereinafter set forth.

The Company agrees to recognize a Department Steward for each of the Divisions or Groups of Employees, as listed in Paragraph A of the Appendix. Should any change in departments or groups of employees, affect a change in the number of stewards, (as listed in Paragraph A of the Appendix) such change in Stewards shall be mutually agreed upon between the representatives of the Company and the Union.

The company will deal with the Department Steward of each Division as hereinafter outlined under the Grievance Procedure. The Company agrees to recognize a Deputy Steward on each night shift to represent his or her department steward. It is agreed that when a Department Steward is absent for any reason, he may appoint a Deputy who shall be recognized in his absence.

This language seems to be a little more particular than the other in that it divides the plant into six sections and appears to make provision for union representatives who hold certain office to function only within their zone or division.

For the most part, the duties of union representatives are understood by the contracting parties, so there are not many agreements which define completely the duties of all the union representatives. Second, this is probably in the interests of the union that views a vague description as permitting a wider latitude of action. However, contracts which embrace very large numbers of workmen often do outline the jurisdictional boundaries within which the various levels of union officials may function. An example of this comes from another UAW contract:

183 (U) Each steward shall represent a particular district (these districts to be established by mutual agreement of the Union and the Company), and shall negotiate grievances only with respect to such districts. After an agreement has been arrived at as to the various districts to be represented by the stewards, the Plant shall not be redistricted more frequently than at six (6) month intervals, except by mutual agreement.

A more simplified version of this is the contractual provision which merely states: "Stewards will be limited to their own departments for settlements of grievances."

In some cases, a more comprehensive definition has apparently been considered beneficial to the parties, probably to aid in minimizing or eliminating possible areas of disagreement. A sample of such detailed coverage comes from a different UAW-organized operation:

189 (U). Stewards are assigned to specific areas in the plant. They are privileged as stewards only within the specific area and are charged with

the responsibility of taking care of grievances within this area only; and will not leave their respective areas during their regular work period without first reporting to an authorized foreman of the area.

Committeemen are assigned to specific zones in the plant. They are privileged as committeemen only within the specific zones, are charged with the responsibility of taking care of grievances which cannot be satisfactorily settled by the stewards who are assigned to the area within the specific zone. Committeemen will not leave their respective zone during the regular working period without first reporting to an authorized foreman of the zone.

The chairman of the bargaining committee, as such, will act as a general committeeman, and will assist the committee members in handling grievances before they reach the bargaining committee. The Chairman of the bargaining committee is charged with the responsibility of taking care of grievances which cannot be satisfactorily settled by the committeemen and superintendent, and will present such grievances to the joint Union Bargaining Committee and Management meeting.

Under an agreement which provided that "union representatives shall be permitted to leave their respective jobs and/or departments when necessary for purpose of investigating or handling grievances," a question arose in arbitration whether the union could appoint a steward to represent employees in a department other than the one in which he worked. In other words, could he represent more than one department? The company declined to recognize the individual who had been appointed steward in any department but his home one. The arbitrator derived controlling guidance from certain contract language. In the relevant portions of this decision, he found the following conditions governing:

> In the current Labor Agreement, the Parties negotiated a new section in Article IX known as Section 5. Neither this or any other similar section was contained in the prior Labor Agreement. It provides that "union representatives shall be permitted to leave their respective jobs *and-or departments* when necessary for the purpose of investigating or handling grievances" [emphasis supplied].
>
> The clear meaning of the new section must be that a departmental steward is authorized, after permission from his supervisor, to go out of his department into another department to conduct grievance handling. . . .
>
> It must be remembered that the Union has the right to conduct its Internal affairs in its own manner and unrestricted by the Company. The Labor Agreement does not authorize the Company to designate who shall be acceptable as departmental representatives; neither does it restrict the operation or appointment of a departmental steward to the department in which he works.

It must, therefore, be the conclusion, based upon the evidence and the provisions of the Labor Agreement, that the appointment of PV as Department Representative of department 90 was made by proper union officials and that she is entitled to serve in that capacity and is further entitled to be recognized by the Company as the duly appointed departmental representative of her constituents in department 90.[1]

Another example of how questions of "representation recognition" have been answered by arbitrators is a case with Corry-Jamestown Corporation and the IAM heard and decided by Arbitrator Samuel S. Kates.[2] Under a contract stating that employees "shall be represented by a department committee of not more than three employees in each department" and that employees might bring a department committeeman into the first step of the grievance procedure, an employee in a department for which the union had designated no committeeman was ruled not to be entitled to have the union president, who worked in another department, represent him in such first-step discussions with the foreman. In the absence of a showing that no employee in the department was capable of action as a committeeman, this was the holding. It was ruled that while the company may have no right ordinarily to tell the union who shall represent the employees, three factors here were controlling: (1) The contract language indicated it was the parties' intention that committeemen should have special knowledge of the activities and problems of the departments they represent. (2) A specific reference to precise situations in which the union president might as a committeeman indicate that he might not adopt that role under ordinary circumstances. (3) The union's prompt compliance with prior requests to furnish lists of department committeemen indicated a recognition of the employer's right to demand designation of department committeemen among employees of the department to be represented.

Commenting on the existence of union offices under an agreement and the conditions which gave rise to them, an arbitrator put it this way:

> Stewardships were created by agreement of the parties. They were devised to implement the bargaining procedures established under the agreement entered into by the parties as a result of the certification of the National Labor Relations Board. They were not created by the certification of the Board.
>
> Since stewardships are creatures of the Agreement of the parties, it is necessary to look to the agreement to determine their responsibilities, duties and rights. Stewards can act only to the extent as provided in the agreement. On the other hand, their activities may not be limited in a manner that would prevent their exercising the rights given them under the

agreement. In other words, the jurisdiction of stewards is no greater or less than that given them under the agreement. The general rights of, and the restrictions covering stewards came into being in the same manner and by the same documents, to wit, the agreements of the parties, as did the rights and the restrictions relating to this Appeal Board and its Chairman.[3]

The setting in which these remarks occurred was under an agreement between Chrysler and the UAW. This collective bargaining agreement established plant "districts" within which department or district stewards functioned. However, a crew of roving inspectors who were home based in a given "district" actually performed their work in several other departments of the plant. Also, some such inspectors performed their tasks in another location apart from the main plant in a facility popularly known by the parties as the Briggs Plant. A district steward who was located and performed his work in the home-base district of these roving inspectors was forbidden by the company to go to the other departments and the Briggs Plant to represent these roving inspectors in union affairs, grievances, and affiliated problems.

The controlling language of the agreement established districts within the plant within which elected union representatives were empowered to carry on legitimate union affairs. The Briggs Plant was not specified in the agreement as an established district. The agreement appeared to limit such union functionaries to executing their duties within the plant areas exclusive of this Briggs Plant. In deciding the question of the right of this district steward to representation in this other area, the arbitrator said: "Since a steward has not been given the right by the parties and the labor agreement to go outside of his district, since the district must be defined as including its physical boundaries, and since there has been no showing that the Briggs Plant is physically within this steward's district #22, the arbitrator must find that the steward has not been given the fight by the parties to investigate grievances at the Briggs Plant."

Under a contract granting union committeemen top seniority in their zones for purposes of "layoffs," an arbiter held the employer did not have a right to transfer a union committeeman to a job outside of his zone on the basis of his actual plant seniority. This was so despite a company contention that such a transfer out of the zone was not a "layoff" per se. A contract provision obstructed the transfer path. Although a transfer is ordinarily not considered a layoff, to have ruled otherwise would have defeated the clear purpose of the contractual provision granting committeemen top seniority. This language served the purposes of (1) protecting the employees' right to representation by individuals of their own choice and (2) preserving the continuity of the union's administrative structure.[4]

In the above-mentioned situation the contractual coverage provided a form of security to union officials to guarantee their retention within their established "areas of stewardship." It works both ways. On the one hand, it ensures to management the scope and limitations of the union representatives' jurisdictional boundaries; on the other hand, it preserves and protects the security of his position while he holds office in that area.

Arbitrators have even ruled that certain union stewards and individual employees were not the proper parties to file grievances because the submitted girevances dealt with matters which occurred in "area," "districts," or "departments" outside the geographical limitations contractually proscribed for the union steward. This happened in a case between North American Aviation and the UAW. This dispute started when the company changed the shift starting time of department 71 from 5:30 P.M. to 4:30 P.M. The contract provided that the regular starting time for the three operating shifts would be 8:00 A.M. for the first shift, 5:30 P.M. for the second shift, and 1:00 A.M. for the third shift. The regulating language which governed the limitation within which the company could change such shift starting times stated: "The company may make such changes in the starting time of shifts provided that such changes *do not* result in the regular shift starting hours specified being changed *more than one half hour from the regular starting times listed.* A change of more than one half hour from the regular starting times listed *may be made only by mutual agreement* between the company and the union."

An examination of the fact situation revealed that the company did change the shift starting time by one hour and that no prior agreement with the union had been obtained. No employee or union representative who worked within the plant district on the shift where the starting times were changed processed any grievance. However, a steward in department 1 on the day shift did file a grievance. The company took the position that this grievant was not a proper party to file a grievance since he was neither directly affected by the change in starting hours nor the steward who represented employees in department 71.

The employer further argued that the practice of the parties as well as the language of the contract prohibited this grievant from filing this grievance. Turning his attention to the contractual grievance procedure and its wording, which the company referred to for its defense, the arbiter concluded that a careful study revealed that grievances were divided into two kinds. Regarding the first type, the contract provided that

"An *individual employee* may present *his* grievance either orally or in writing to his foreman."

It was significant to the arbitrator to note that this clause did not say "*a* grievance" but "*his* grievance." The second type provided for under the grievance procedure of this agreement allowed the district steward the right to investigate and "present to a foreman *in his district* a grievance on behalf of the union when he has facts indicating a violation of the agreement has occurred *in this district.*"

In view of contract language and after satisfying himself that the company had consistently followed a policy of processing grievances only on behalf of employees directly affected by alleged violations from within the actual districts in which the violations occurred, the arbitrator ruled:

> It is uncontradicted that B [the steward and individual filing the grievance] was working in another department on another shift. He was therefore not affected by the change in the starting time of the shift. On the basis of the above reasoning, he therefore could not properly file a grievance against the company's alleged violation of the contract. Inasmuch as he was not the steward in the district involved, he was not the proper party to file a grievance under Article V. Section 14C. Only the district steward in Dept. 71, or the zone committeeman in that steward's absence, could file such a grievance.... The arbitrator therefore cannot rule on its merits.[5]

Notes

Chapter 1

1. 39 LA 238.
2. 33 LA 146.
3. 33 LA 701.
4. 15 LA 842.
5. 44 LA 453.
6. 48 LA 203, Arbitrator Alexander B. Porter.
7. 41 LA 1288.
8. 43 LA 46.
9. 8 LA 826.
10. 16 LA 307.
11. 27 LA 400.
12. 40 LA 549.
13. 1 LA 155.
14. 11 LA 462.
15. 13 LA 143.
16. 12 LA 238.
17. 4 LA 403.
18. 21 LA 421.
19. 20 LA 875.
20. 46 LA 275.
21. 43 LA 838.
22. 44 LA 604.
23. 30 LA 820.
24. 47 LA 370.
25. 16 LA 307.
26. 38 LA 82.
27. 14 LA 925.

Chapter 2

1. 1 LA 423.
2. 10 LA 260.

3. 10 LA 43.

4. 3 LA 598.

5. 40 LA 201.

6. 48 LA 1345.

7. 49 LA 209.

8. 10 LA 786.

9. 14 LA 55.

10. 41 LA 1053, Arbitrator Joseph Shister. For a case with a similar finding, see 24 LA 703.

11. 15 LA 65.

12. 15 LA 652.

13. 13 LA 545.

14. 39 LA 567.

15. 50 LA 1140.

16. 36 LA 503.

17. 17 LA 230.

18. 21 LA 67. For similar case, see 15 LA 652, 10 LA 786, and 3 LA 721.

19. 33 LA 667, Arbitrator Robert G. McIntosh.

20. 3 LA 374.

21. 35 LA 621.

22. 50 LA 634, Arbitrator David L. Kabaker.

23. See *Industrial Relations—Union Contracts—Collective Bargaining* (Prentice-Hall).

24. 21 LA 220, Arbitrator Harry H. Platt.

Chapter 3

1. 35 LA 228.

2. For a review of such cases, see 36 LA 291, Arbitrator Marion Beatty; 36 LA 351, Arbitrator Arthur Stark; and 35 LA 228, Arbitrator Sylvester Garret.

3. This view expressed in 36 LA 297.

4. For arbitration rulings interposing this defense under Section 302, see 10 LA 471, 36 LA 351.

5. 39 LA 393, Arbitrator Sidney L. Cahn.

6. 35 LA 228, Arbitrator Harry J. Dworkin.

7. 35 LA 228.

8. 64-1, ARB-8151.

9. 28 LA 107.

10. 44 LA 824.

11. 41 LA 1042.

12. For other examples, see 35 LA 699, 48 LA 164, 40 LA 548, 32 LA 719, 34 LA 332, 31 LA 617.

13. *Aerovox Corporation* (1953), 102 NLRB 1526, supplemented on other issues, 104 NLRB 246, enforced (D.C. Cir. 1954), 211 F.2d 640, 33 LRRM 2437, *cert. denied* 347 U.S. 968, 98 L. Ed. 1109, 74 Sup. Ct. 774, 34 LRRM 2143 (1954).

14. *General Shoe Corporation* (1950), 90 NLRB 1330, *enforced* (6th Cir. 1951), 192 F.2d 504, 29 LRRM 2112, *cert. denied,* 343 U.S. 904, 96 L. Ed. 1323, 72 Sup. Ct. 634, 29 LRRM 2606 (1952).

15. 34 LA 55.

16. 34 LA 731.

17. 34 LA 858.

18. 17 LA 623.

19. 50 LA 909.

20. 44 LA 917.

21. 46 LA 920.

22. 46 LA 637.

23. 50 LA 1025.

Chapter 4

1. 23 LA 317.

2. 10 LA 487.

3. 48 LA 524.

4. 41 LA 1053.

5. 44 LA 544.

6. 42 LA 1267.

7. *Republic Aviation Corporation v. NLRB,* 324 U.S. 793, 16 LRRM 620.

8. 8 LA 891.

9. 30 LA 358.

10. 40 LA 476.

11. 32 LA 223.

12. 47 LA 858, 16 LA 229, 17 LA 829, 28 LA 363, 26 LA 105, 25 LA 472.

13. 47 LA 858.

14. 42 LA 576.

15. *Aluminum Ore Co. v. NLRB,* 131 F.2d 485, 6LC-61332, (CA-7 1942).

16. *NLRB v. Southland Cork Co.,* 342 F.2d 702, 51 LC-19567, (CA-4 1965); *Weinacker Bros. Inc.,* 153 NLRB No. 40, 1965 CCH, NLRB-9478.

17. *Fafnir Bearing Co.,* 14 NLRB 1582 (1964).

18. *Metropolitan Life Insurance Company,* 150 NLRB 135 (1965).

19. *Fafnir Bearing Co.,* (UAW) 146 NLRB 1582 (1964).

20. 136 NLRB 1648 (1962).

21. *Celotex Corp.,* 146 NLRB 48 (1964); *Ingalls Shipbuilding Corp.,* 143 NLRB 712 (1963); Administrative Decision of General Counsel, 1963 CCH-NLRB-12,657, Case. No. SR-2595.

22. See cases cited below. For summary, see LRX *(Labor Relations Expediter),* "Collective Bargaining," Sec. 19. Compare *NLRB v. Truitt Mfg. Co.,* 351 U.S. 149, 38 LRRM 2042 (1956).

23. *Otis Elevator Co.,* 102 NLRB 770, 31 LRRM 1334, 33 LRRM 2129.

24. *Otis Elevator Co., supra,* arose from a grievance. See also *General Con-*

trols Co., 88 NLRB 1341, 25 LRRM 1475, and *NLRB v. New Britain Machine Co.,* 33 LRRM 2461.

25. 36 LRRM 220, 35 LRRM 2215, 35 LRRM 2730, 27 LRRM 2524-25-26.

26. 10 LRRM 49, 11 LRRM 693, 36 LRRM 2220.

27. 72 LRRM 1113.

28. 362 F.2d 716, 62 LRRM 2415 (2CIR. 19866).

29. In support of this finding, the court cited *International Union of Electrical, Radio and Machine Workers v. General Electric Co.,* 332 F.2d 485, 56 LRRM 2289 (2 CIR) *cert. den.,* 379 U.S. 928, 57 LRRM 2608 (1964).

30. Case No. 17-CA-3543, 175 NLRB 19 (1969), 70 LRRM 1490.

31. Case No. 21-CA-7917, 174 NLRB 11 (1969) 70 LRRM 1072; 65 LRRM 1509 and 69 LRRM 1409.

Chapter 5

1. 27 LA 148.
2. 38 LA 1226.
3. 52 LA 61.
4. 18 LA 772.
5. 47 LA 672.
6. 35 LA 506.
7. 49 LA 346.
8. 45 LA 612.
9. 41 LA 360.
10. 15 LA 895.
11. 44 LA 858.
12. 24 LA 313.
13. *State v. Powell,* 61 ALR 966 (DEL 1904).
14. 10 LA 675.
15. 46 LA 956.
16. 2 LA 534, *Northwestern Foundry Co. v. UAW.*
17. 8 LA 688.
18. 17 LA 710, *Reynolds Metals Co. v. USW.*
19. 8 LA 648. For a related case, see 6 LA 58. See also 27 LA 557. For a different treatment of a similar problem, see 10 LA 637.
20. 21 LA 327.
21. 31 LA 675.
22. 39 LA 248.
23. 26 LA 480.
24. 29 LA 451.
25. 27 LA 557.
26. 24 LA 603.
27. 28 LA 434.
28. 20 LA 175, 28 LA 434.

Chapter 6

1. 3 LA 779; see also 6 LA 447, 19 LA 43.
2. 9 LA 861; For a decision that this principle does not apply to "action falling primarily within the union's domain," see Shulman in 10 LA 213.
3. 63-1 ARB-8012.
4. 21 LA 410.
5. 7 LA 3.
6. 11 LA 456.
7. 6 LA 988.
8. 44 LA 141.
9. 21 LA 410.

Chapter 7

1. 45 LA 1124.
2. J. Gross, in 20 LA 749; see also 2 LA 295.
3. 34 LA 332.
4. J. Justin, in 10 LA 255. For other cases where discipline was imposed upon union representatives while "acting as an employee," see 15 LA 842, 1 LA 447, 9 LA 765, 43 LA 46, 33 LA 701. For a contrary opinion, see 17 LA 199.
5. W. McCoy, in 15 LA 307; see also 39 LA 238, 30 LA 143.
6. 21 LA 239.
7. 39 LA 1080.
8. D. Whiting, in 10 LA 965.
9. *Sivyer Steel Casting Cmopany v. UAW,* 30 LA 41.
10. 34 LA 464; see also 10 LA 372 for a similar case. For a contrary decision, see 33 LA 146.
11. *Chrysler Corporation v. UAW,* 33 LA 879.
12. 10 LA 75.
13. 10 LA 660.
14. H. Platt, in 21 LA 10; for a similar case, see 14 LA 925.
15. Updegraff, in 10 LA 355; see also 9 LA 861.
16. 42 LA 923.
17. 43 LA 76.
18. 49 LA 1189.

Chapter 8

1. 4 LA 744, 21 LA 421, 16 LA 99, 21 LA 843, 9 LA 447, 13 LA 304, 30 LA 181, 30 LA 250.
2. 28 LA 369; see also 35 LA 6990, 20 LA 875, 33 LA 488, 6 LA 414.
3. 28 LA 782; see also 16 LA 99, 29 LA 622, 43 LA 608, 8 LA 758, 30 LA 109, 30 LA 562, 20 LA 250, 34 LA 325, 34 LA 607, 33 LA 594, 13 LA 143, 6 LA 617, 13 LA 295, 14 LA 475, 7 LA 648; for a contrary view, see 33 LA 807.

4. 31 LA 675.

5. Joseph M. Klamon, in 38 LA 928. For a similar decision, see Arbitrator Harold J. Davey, in 39 LA 1144.

6. 43 LA 1070.

7. 44 LA 942.

8. 42 LA 131.

9. 50 LA 1157.

10. 50 LA 562.

11. 47 LA 129.

12. 41 LA 609.

13. 6 LA 799.

14. 41 LA 1240.

15. 45 LA 943.

16. 47 LA 1100.

17. *Grievance Handling: 101 Guides for Supervisors,* W. Baer. A.M.A., 1971.

18. Philip G. Marshall, in 38 LA 889; see also Arbitrator Monroe Berkowitz, in 38 LA 986 and 38 LA 705.

19. 33 LA 807.

Chapter 9

1. 168 NLRB 84, 66 LRRM 1353 (1967).

2. 172 NLRB 84, 68 LRRM 1305 (1968).

3. 68 LRRM 1305.

4. 56 LRRM 1071.

5. 72 LRRM 1245.

6. 52 LA 1078.

7. 27 LA 892.

8. 27 LA 895.

Chapter 10

1. 50 LA 634.

2. 36 LA 682.

3. 50 LA 637.

4. 22 LA 535.

5. 22 LA 540.

Index

147